Stephen Port, Serial Killer

Pete Dove

Published by Trellis Publishing, 2021.

While every precaution has been taken in the preparation of this book, the publisher assumes no responsibility for errors or omissions, or for damages resulting from the use of the information contained herein.

STEPHEN PORT, SERIAL KILLER

First edition. July 1, 2021.

Copyright © 2021 Pete Dove.

ISBN: 979-8224263271

Written by Pete Dove.

STEPHEN PORT, SERIAL KILLER

pete DOVE

STEPHEN PORT
When Prejudice Leads to Death

'That's what gay men do. They take drugs and die in graveyards.'

This angry, ironic statement was uttered with absolute bitterness by John Pape, friend of a victim of one of Britain's most horrific serial killers. He had good reason to make it.

But our story begins, in many ways, with its end. That this is so is hugely to the discredit of a British law enforcement unit. The Metropolitan police refused to investigate a series of murders, insisting that each death was suicide or accidental. Yet they were so obviously related that it is hard to see how the London force could miss the links between them.

It was September 14th 2015 when Jack Taylor, a 25 year old gay man was found dead in St Margaret's church in East London. 'If that's where Jack's been found, someone's put him there,' said Jack's sister, Jen. 'The Police could have put a stop to it, and Jack would still have been here.'

Three previous murders had been committed in 2014. In each case, a body was found within a short distance of the others – sometimes in the exact same spot. Yet police assumed there was no connection between the crimes. It was only after the discovery of Jack's body that investigators realised they had a serial killer on their hands.

Earlier that month, Jack made contact with the man who would go on to poison him on the gay dating site, Grindr. That person was Stephen Port, a forty year old Chef who lived in Barking, East London.

When Jack went missing, his family were in an immediate panic. 'We were all trying to get hold of him, explained Jen. 'We were chasing up his friends.'

His other sister, Donna, takes up the story. Two days after his parents had reported Jack missing she got another update from her mom and dad. The news was non-committal – there was no more information about her brother's whereabouts. But even as they were talking on the phone a police car pulled up outside. Donna heard the words she had feared through the echo of her cell, her mum screaming in the background.

Jack was dead. He had been found propped up in the churchyard, nearby lay evidence of drug use, and among this paraphernalia police discovered an open bottle of the drug GHB, a substance associated with raucous parties. Jack had consumed an overdose, and this is what had killed him.

It was easy for the police to deduce that the young man had killed himself, deliberately or by accident. But his family knew that this was an impossibility.

'Jack was very anti-drugs, so that did not make sense,' argued Donna. The family shared a gut feeling which kept surfacing above their grief. Something about Jack's death was simply not right.

We will see later that the Metropolitan Police really do not come out well in the entire case of Stephen Port. Two weeks after he was found, Jack's family were still pestering police for more information. Finally, some CCTV footage they had was shared. It showed Jack meeting up with an older man. It was the early hours of the morning, an unusual time to meet a friend.

The older man in the footage was, of course, Stephen Port.

Port had been born in the seaside town of Southend on Sea in 1975. But the family moved to nearby London when he was still a baby. Dagenham might not enjoy the various joys and attractions of the Thames Estuary as Southend does, but offered wider employment opportunities. However, this East End borough is far from the most salubrious part of London. It does not feature widely on the tourist routes through England's capital city. Back in the mid-seventies, it was an even more challenging place. During Stephen Port's early years, the area was dominated by the Ford Motor Car works, the major blue collar employer in the district; it was a rough, tough working class region of London.

Criminologist Dr Elizabeth Yardley has looked into Port's early years. She concludes that the future killer's upbringing was remarkable only its in unremarkability. He lived in a traditional working class home, with working class parents. From the evidence available, they were caring, hard working people.

Nothing strange grabs our attention to offer a reason why the boy became the man he did. As a child Stephen was quiet, and found it hard to make conversation with others. For a while, his teachers even considered that he might be deaf, so much in his own world did he live.

But that in itself is not unusual. Children can be withdrawn for many reasons – lack of self-esteem, because of problems at home, or at school. Gender dysphoria is a field we are beginning to learn much more about. But we are only speculating if we attach any of these conditions to Stephen. Autism is a spectrum into which many people fall. A lack of social understanding, delayed emotional development, an inability to empathise, a difficulty in relating to one's peers – these are all symptoms of this damaging condition. From some of the evidence of his later life, this seems a more reasonable hypothesis to draw when we seek to explain his crimes. Yet, once more, we cannot be sure.

However, nothing seems to have occurred in Stephen Port's childhood to explain the savage person he would become. Perhaps that is because, in the early eighties while Port was in school, little was known about the symptoms and consequences of autism.

Like most of his peers, Stephen took his examinations at sixteen. In those days, a two tier system operated, with the brighter kids taking the gold standard O levels, while those with less apparent ability sat the easier CSEs. Although, social class was often a clearer indicator of which exams a child sat than actual intellect. The education system in Britain in the 1970s was firmly determined to maintain the status quo.

Those with the best exam results over-whelmingly came from wealthy, middle class backgrounds, while the working class kids were far more likely to be pushed towards the lesser valued CSE route. That meant that post school education for the middle classes was most likely to be university, with a place fully funded by the state. Meanwhile for those most in need of support to better themselves, their CSE exams were unlikely to secure a seat at a university. Therefore, they would be forced either into work (or, more likely, unemployment) or to a college – a less academic and prestigious place of learning.

At best, in most cases, such a path would only be partially funded. Like many of his generation, Stephen chose the latter of these two routes – art college in his case – but his working class family were unable to meet his fees and other costs, and he was forced to leave.

Still, Stephen was bestowed with a traditional lower class protestant worth ethic, and although the route he chose after leaving art school was not one he would prefer, nevertheless he was determined to do the best he could for himself. He trained to be a chef.

Dr Yardley sees this move as significant in the emergence of him as a murderer. She claims that Stephen Port carried forward a resentment of being forced into a career that he did not want to follow. He is, she argues, also frustrated that his talent for art does not get an opportunity to be fully explored. Perhaps she is right, or perhaps Port should be commended for overcoming the iniquities of an extremely unfair educational system that writes off many young people before they have the chance to shine.

Port lived with his parents until he reached the age of thirty. Affording one's own home is not a very realistic prospect for a young man living in London, even the generally less expensive East End. This is particularly the case when working in a relatively low paid job such as a chef.

However, he did move out when he reached thirty, renting a flat in Cooke Street, Barking - a borough both similar and adjacent to Dagenham

Ensconced alone in his first home, he soon became friendly with a neighbour, Ryan Edwards. He too was new to the area in 2005, when both moved into the block. Ryan noticed that Port was a 'man of few words.'

'He often would not give eye contact,' he said. Ryan also noted the awkward, almost lumbering stride of the tall man. It was as though Stephen Port was uncomfortable in his own body.

Ryan recalls another incident which suggests that Port had not developed emotionally as many other adults do. On this occasion, Ryan hosted a party to which Port was invited. The host had found a toy truck on the pavement and presented it to his neighbour, much to the surprise of some of the other guests.

Port was delighted, and shifted his large frame to the carpet, where he sat cross legged playing with the toy. This was not Stephen Port playing to the crowd. He was in his own world, genuinely enjoying the toy.

This was not unusual behaviour for Stephen Port. In his flat, police later discovered a large collection of children's toys which the adult played with as though still a boy. Clearly, some part of his emotional development had been stunted.

He seemed to be unfazed by how such behaviour might be regarded by others around him. But if Stephen found establishing and maintaining relationships extremely difficult in real, face to face situations, modern society had given birth to a means by which he could do so on his own terms. Social media. It was through this medium that Port could operate on his terms, in his own space.

Social media also allowed him to hide behind multiple personae. On the numerous profiles he established using a range of platforms he variously claimed to be ex-military, an Oxbridge graduate, a special needs teacher.

It seems as though Stephen was more at home with these false identities than with his real self. The result was that killer to be met a host of new men, each of whom he considered as his boyfriend.

'He would contact me, usually by text,' recalls Ryan Edwards 'and say "I've got a new boyfriend. Come round and meet my new boyfriend."'

Sometimes these relationships would change daily. Perhaps it was the lies he told online that put off each new man in his life. Seemingly afraid that what he was would fail to attract the men he wanted, Port would publish photos of himself as a much younger man.

The men to whom he was attracted were always young. Psychiatrists conclude that the reason for this was that he lacked confidence being around men of his own age; however, with younger partners he felt more in control, and therefore more confident.

Likely as well, he felt younger in his mind – much younger – than he really was. But he consumed partners voraciously, rarely letting relationships develop. It was as though he had an appetite for vulnerable young men.

But this appetite was not easily satiated. Ryan Edwards recalls that often Port would leave his visitors with him, and they would chat. Few, he recalls, had a good word for the lanky chef. They saw him as controlling, argumentative and difficult. He wanted, needed, to be in control. It worked sometimes, and the men he targeted would hang around longer than usual. He did seem to possess a gift for sniffing out the most vulnerable young gay men in East London.

Port's searches took him further afield, and he became involved in drug ridden sex parties. He kept vials of GHB, packets of cocaine in his home. It was when Ryan Edwards discovered this – Port was neither discreet nor secretive about some things – that he realised this was a friendship from which he might be best to back away.

Living alone, nothing was in place to act as a break on the chef's behaviour. The result was that his relationships became ever more violent, ever more dangerous and excessively controlling. His fantasies were beginning to turn to a frightening reality, and when they did, the deaths began.

When police later examined the search history on his computer even hardened officers were shocked by the depravity on which he was hooked. The images and films he was watching might have offered some satisfaction in the beginning, but soon Port needed more. He needed to be actively involved in the kind of sick and perverted actions that attracted him.

This shows the confusion in the quiet man's head. On the one hand, he liked to play with toy cars, on the other he was attracted by the vilest of sexual deviancy.

And so, inevitably, his desires moved from the abstract to the actual. He met up with a twenty three year old fashion student, Anthony Walgate, through a male escort site. It was June 15th 2014 and Port offered Walgate £800 to spend the night with him. Anthony agreed, but texted friends to tell them about the arrangement. They planned to meet on the 17th, and two days after that Anthony was found dead outside the entrance to Port's flat.

It seems as though the chef believed that his escort for the night was not dead, because he phoned the emergency services anonymously to report what had happened. Or, at least, his version of it.

'Cooke Street. There's a young boy who looks like he's collapsed outside,' he tells the emergency services operator. 'Looks like he's collapsed, or had a seizure or something. Or just drunk.'

The ambulance found Anthony propped up against a wall. Beside him was his rucksack, and inside this a bottle of GHB – the drug commonly used on date rapes. He was later found to have died of an overdose of the substance. Police didn't see anything suspicious in the death.

But then came a mistake that is hard to explain away, and would lead to the deaths of at least three more young men.

Anthony's mother was convinced that her son would not overdose on purpose. To her, something inexplicable had happened. But the police were not interested. The boy's body bore no obvious signs of assault, and they had decided upon the cause of death. Cynics might argue that, to their eyes, this was just another young man involved in a promiscuous lifestyle who had either misjudged the effects of a cocktail of drugs or who had decided that his life had fallen to such a low that he had to end it.

But Anthony's friends, like his mother, saw no truth in this interpretation. They contacted police and reported that he had told them he was meeting a man on the evening he died. It took police little time to realise that this was the same man who had phoned through to the emergency services that night. If, at this stage, Stephen Port's actions made him a criminal, he was an extremely inept one indeed.

Port was arrested, his flat searched and his laptop taken. He concocted a story which, incredibly, police believed. He said that Anthony had taken drugs and fallen asleep. Port had then gone to work and discovered his new friend dead when he returned later in the day. He had panicked, and carried the body downstairs and left it outside the apartment block. Port was released and, having been so close to being discovered, was filled with a new lease of life. To somebody with his fragile mental state, he must have felt immortal.

However, he had not got away scot free with his actions. Police charged him with the relatively minor offence of perverting the course of justice, and he was due for trial in March 2015. Believing his story, they failed to examine his laptop and phone in any kind of detail, and as a result missed vital clues that might have indicated his crime was more serious than a technical one.

Within a couple of months, Port was back on Grindr. He made contact with a 21 year old Slovakian, Gabriel Kovari. It was Gabriel's former flat mate, John Pape who uttered the angry quote at the beginning of this report, and would ultimately play a major role in the capture of Port. Gabriel was a friendly, intelligent young man, an aspiring artist with a true passion for the subject.

Ryan Edwards met him. He invited he and Port back to his flat for coffee. The older man left the room for the toilet, and Gabriel revealed a truth Ryan already suspected. 'Stephen is not the man we think he is,' said the young artist. 'He is a bad man.'

Gabriel was not the typical person Stephen tended to hook up with. He was a young man with a clear purpose, one who had an aim in life. Possibly, this self-assuredness threatened Port, who liked his young men to be docile so he could dominate them. Ryan and Gabriel became friends, and stayed in touch through social media during the few days he had left alive.

But suddenly the messages stopped. Ryan was worried, and contacted Stephen. The stories he heard over the following days were inconsistent. Firstly, Port said that Gabriel had just left but he did not know to where he had gone. Then, that he had teamed up with a soldier, and moved in with him. Next, Port expressed worry about Gabriel's safety and finally told Ryan, via a long text message, that Gabriel had in fact headed home to Slovakia, but that he had contacted a sudden and severe illness and had tragically died. At least the final part of that package of lies was true.

In fact, on August 28th, just five days after moving in with Port, Gabriel had been found, dead. A woman walking her dog had come across his body propped up in St Margaret's Churchyard. Once more, it seemed as though this was a young man killed by a drugs overdose. But police made no connection with the death of another young homosexual man three months earlier.

For the partly child-like Stephen, this is like a small boy getting away with stealing sugar from the food cupboard. He remains undiscovered, nobody tells him to stop, so he carries on. And rather like the small child, he both gains in confidence, and discovers his appetite for his nefarious acts is growing.

By the eighteenth of September he is active once more. Still on bail awaiting proceedings for the charge of perverting the course of justice, he contacted another twenty one year old, Daniel Whitworth. Just as Gabriel had shared Port's passion for art, so Daniel shared an interest with the older man. He too was a chef.

It was only two days later that his body was discovered, once more in the graveyard at St Margaret's church. He was even in the same spot and remarkably, horrifically, was discovered by the same woman walking her dog. Did police make the connection? No.

Once more, the authorities made the assumption that Daniel had committed suicide, They had, though, an excuse for doing this. A suicide note was found on his body which claimed that Daniel had killed himself because he was filled with guilt for murdering Gabriel three weeks before. Presumably, it would take only the slightest investigation to find that this was not the case, and to make a link back to Stephen Port. That investigation did not take place.

But despite the complacency of the police, Daniel's stepmother would not accept the picture they painted. Eventually, she saw the letter and realised that it was not the work of her young stepson.

She also spotted within it something so naively obvious that it shouted out at her as raising concern. Allegedly, Daniel had written: 'Don't blame the man I was with last night, that was only sex.' To her, the question of who this man might be was of crucial importance, although it did not seem so to the officers investigating the case.

Their inaction poses an obvious question. How might the police have investigated if the victims had been women, or middle class heterosexual males, or older people? That they were young, gay boys seems to have clouded the police force's eyes to what was happening in their patch.

But if nothing was raising questions in the eyes of the authorities, news that three young men had all apparently died of a drug overdose in Barking over the course of just a few months was causing ripples in the LGBT community.

John Pape tried to take some action. Peter Tatchell is a high profile gay rights campaigner with a regular media presence in the UK. Pape contacted him.

'I was shocked that the police had issued no public appeal, and there seemed to be no on-going investigation,' said the campaigner. He advised John Pape to contact both Pink News, a leading gay website, and the body who monitor police actions in the UK, but both were assured by the authorities that they had looked into the matter, and there was nothing to find.

Then, on March 23rd Port was sentenced to eight months in prison for perverting the course of justice, a charge to which he pleaded guilty. Two months later, in June 2015, he was released. And free to strike again. He did not wait long.

On September 15th 2015, another body was found in exactly the same churchyard as Gabriel and Daniel. That was Jack Taylor.

The fork lift driver's family were not prepared to be put off by police inaction or assumptions. They knew that Jack would not wander into a lonely cemetery late at night. 'He was scared of the dark,' explained his sister Donna, simply. Such a basic contradiction encouraged them to press the police for CCTV footage, and soon Jack was spotted accompanying a tall, blond man.

A month later police appealed to the public for the identity of the man, and Stephen Port was quickly identified. It really was as simple as that. Port was not a master criminal. He possessed all the unsubtle guile of the child he really was. His attempts at diverting police attention did more to attract it than succeed in putting it off. His fortune in coming across an investigating department who seemed to hold little interest in finding the truth was the only reason he was able to kill four times.

A month after Jack's body was discovered, with his family refusing to let the police off the hook, Port was arrested once more. This time he was charged with the murder of four young men.

Finally, his computer was properly searched. The footage of him having sex with unconscious young men was incriminating. So too was his search history seeking out footage of drug fuelled rapes.

And so, in November 20sixteen, Port appeared at the Old Bailey. He was convicted of four murders, and numerous other rapes, sexual assaults and the administration of drugs. Eleven men were involved as victims all told. He was sentenced to life in prison, with a recommendation that he never be released.

But the story did not stop there. The following year, the BBC released a documentary about the police investigation into Port's crimes. The matter had only reached criminal proceedings thanks to the determination of John Pape and Jack Taylor's family, despite the coroner who reported on Daniel's death raising significant questions about the police's action.

Seventeen police officers were investigated by the police complaints commission, and the families of the victims have launched a civil case against the Metropolitan Police. Indications are that the report will be damming, but it cannot be released until after a second inquest is held into the deaths of all four of the young men. That will happen later in 2019.

The reaction of the victim's families and friends to the news that the truth was coming out was varied yet, in each case, equally tragic. Sarah Sak is Anthony Walgate's mother. 'I felt like I had been shot,' she explained when hearing that Port had been arrested and charged.

Jack's sisters Donna and Jen experienced a numbness; a sense that they had contributed to the facts coming out, but also horror that should a truth should be there. John Pape, Gabriel's friend, was in Kathmandu when detectives contacted him to explain that they had arrested Port on suspicion of his former flat mate's death. For him there was a feeling of anger and loneliness. A frustration that a life had been wasted needlessly.

Daniel Whitworth's mother experienced the strangest, most obscure and disturbing reaction to hearing that her step son's killer had been caught. It was one of relief, pleasure almost, that her boy had not killed himself.

He had not fallen to a place so dark that he had been unable to reach out for help, and instead had taken his own life. Soon, that emotion was replaced by anger. Such are the consequences for the families of murder victims. But in Daniel's case, along with Jack Taylor and Gabriel Kovari, they were victims whose deaths should have been avoided... had the police not failed to do their job.

For many years, certain police forces in the UK were known for being institutionally racist. Improvements have been made on that front, although many would argue that these have not gone far enough. The fear must now exist that, for some forces at least, a charge of institutional homophobia might reasonably be applied.

MISSING BETHANY: THE TRUE STORY OF BETHANY DECKER

15

JENNY GREENWOOD

In many ways the life of Bethany Decker was not so different from others her age and who shared similar backgrounds. She worked full time as a waitress and attended college at George Mason University, majoring in Global Environmental Change. Sure, she was only 22 and married with one son, just 17-months-old. But that is hardly uncommon. And yes, her marriage was faltering, but even that was hardly unique, especially when married at such a young age to a husband serving repeated tours of duty in Afghanistan.

Nothing about Bethany seemed out of the ordinary.

Until she disappeared.

On January 29th, 2011 the young wife and mother vanished and has not been seen since.

What happened to Bethany Decker?

At the time of her disappearance, Bethany and her husband, Emile Decker had been married for 18 months. Their son was living with Bethany's mother, Kim Nelson, while Bethany focused on finishing her last semester at George Mason.

"She is my flip flops and lip gloss girl," her mother said, giving her that nickname because she was born in Hawaii. Bethany was a terrific student and graduated from high school with a 4.0 GPA. At the time of her disappearance she was only just a few credits shy of graduating from George Mason University. Her studies by day and her hard work as a waitress by night was about to pay off. With her degree she hoped to change the world in a positive way.

"Bethany was a physically attractive young woman," forensic psychologist Tim McGee said. "She was petite at four-foot-eleven and weighed 130 pounds. She was curvy and had a pretty face. Surely, she had more than her share of men who wanted to date her. Invariably, she attracted men who would be uncomfortable with dating someone who got a lot of attention from rivals."

As days and weeks passed with no contact, her family said they didn't begin to worry right away since the 21-year-old had such a hectic schedule. With Bethany away at college and working full-time it had not concerned her mother that she had not heard from her daughter in over three weeks. She tried calling on several occasions and was just directed to her voice-mail box.

"She had a seventeen-month old child at the time," McGee said. "But the child would stay with her in-laws. Still, those days where no one heard from her would suggest that they were used to not having her checking-in. So there is the possibility that there was some estrangement there."

Kim Nelson was not the only one struggling to get a hold of Bethany. One weekend Kim received a number of strange phone calls and some of Bethany's friends noticed unusual posts on Bethany's Facebook page.

"It was a Saturday morning and I had messages from four different people from different parts of the country that said, 'there's somebody on Facebook that's on Bethany's login, but it's not Bethany. It didn't sound like Bethany and didn't use terms Bethany would use. What's going on? Is there something wrong?'" Bethany's mother Kim said.

Kim immediately called her own parents to check on Bethany because they lived closer to her apartment in Ashburn, Virginia. Upon arrival, they noticed that Bethany's car was parked crooked, had a flat tire, and was dusty. This was peculiar because her grandparents drove past only one week prior and the car was parked differently.

The unused car, the Facebook posts, and the radio silence from Bethany formed mounting evidence that something was not quite right. But what finally inspired her family to call the police was when her grandparents knocked on her door and heard no answer.

"We just had a feeling. We were concerned," Evelyn Bayles, Bethany's grandmother said.

On February 19, 2011 Bayles called the local police dept. and investigators soon descended upon the apartment complex and interviewed every collateral contact in Bethany's life. But it had been at least three weeks since anyone had seen her. The only trace left behind was her dusty, double-parked car.

The vehicle was searched, but it left no clues as to where she might have disappeared to. Her apartment revealed nothing. It was entirely empty, except for a bag of her own clothes. There were no signs of foul play or a physical altercation. Her bank account had been static for weeks. Soon, the police organized search teams who prowled the nearby landscape with dogs and combed through dumpsters, looking for human remains. She had not shown up for her scheduled shift at Carrabba's Italian Grill in Centreville, VA, the popular restaurant chain where she worked, since the day she was last seen. She had disappeared without a trace.

"We want Bethany safe. We love her and we want to know that she is OK," Bethany's mother said to reporters. An investigator also noted that there was no evidence or indication that Bethany was not alive. But behind the investigator's affirmation, lay the disturbing truth that there was no activity on her bank account, email account, or cell phone records.

SUSPECT THE HUSBAND FIRST

At first, the disappearance seemed like an elaborate ruse engineered by Bethany's husband, Emile. According to police, Emile had seen Bethany the day before she disappeared. And despite finding no activity on her bank account, email account, or cell phone records, someone was still posting on her Facebook account.

Someone had her login information. Who better to suspect than her husband?

The investigators started to circle their wagons around Emile. The motive lined up all-too-well. He was a young man stuck serving in Afghanistan while quietly harboring suspicions that Bethany was being unfaithful. She had become pregnant again but was it even his child? One week before her disappearance, between Jan. 18 to Jan. 23, Bethany and Emile had vacationed in Hawaii in what was possibly a desperate last-ditch attempt to save their marriage. When that failed, the investigators speculated, Emile descended into a fit of rage and Bethany disappeared.

What buttressed this theory was that she was never at the airport to bid him farewell before he returned to Afghanistan on February 2nd 2011. His wife did not see him off, as she had multiple times before, investigators said. His fellow infantrymen thought this was peculiar but attributed it to the marital difficulties that Emile was experiencing.

Armed with this information, investigators were eager to interrogate Emile and did so within a few days of Bethany's disappearance.

"He is cooperating. He's answered several questions for us now," a spokesman for the police said. They did not have details of their conversation with Emile, but said they were trying to establish a more solid time line of when Bethany was last seen based on information from her husband.

But because Emile was serving in Afghanistan by the time the investigation started, investigators needed to contact U.S. military officials to arrange bringing him back home for further questioning and a polygraph test.

But Emile was not being named a suspect or a person of interest in the case.

"I don't want to limit him saying he's a suspect or a person of interest at this time. We're playing catch up on an investigation of a missing person, therefore, we would like to talk to as many people as possible," the police spokesman said.

"He wants to cooperate fully. He was very concerned of Bethany's whereabouts and condition. Obviously, being the father of their child he wants to hear a good resolution to this."

AN AFFAIR AT WORK

Bethany was having an affair with a man named Ronald Roldan, a Bolivian immigrant she met at Carrabba's Italian Grill. With that information, it wasn't inconceivable that the five-months pregnant Bethany was carrying Roldan's child. Investigators now had someone other than Emile with a possible motive in the case.

Roldan would also be the last person to see her in the Ashburn apartment on January 29th, 2011.

The two were reportedly living together in the Orchard Grass Terrace complex until the lease expired on Jan. 31, and from the very beginning, according to friends and family, the relationship was abusive. Bethany Decker met Roldan at a vulnerable time in her life according to her mother. She did not plan on being in a relationship with Roldan, nor staying in a relationship with him. When Nelson first met him, she found him to be charming. But friends and family soon learned that he turned controlling and even dangerous. Friends insisted that she check-in regularly with them as the relationship turned from emotionally abusive to physically abusive.

"The whole circumstance of her getting involved with Roldan is nuts," McGee said. "The media had to be careful not to judge her for behavior in having an affair because then that suggests that she brought on the violence to herself. But it is apparent that her mother knew about the affair."

Bethany had been desperately exploring a safe exit strategy from the relationship, according to her mother. But Roldan refused to leave and he would not let her leave either. She confided to her mother the danger that Roldan posed to her life, saying there was a time when Roldan threw her across the room and into a wall. He threatened to cut her open with car keys. Her family encouraged her to just walk away from the relationship, but she insisted that, "He'll never let it go. He'll find me."

Investigators believe that Bethany was in the Ashburn apartment the day she went missing because she made a commitment to work that evening at Carrabba's Italian Grill, not far away from Ashburn. But she never showed up for her scheduled shift, thus making Roldan the last person to see her that day.

In March 2011, only a few weeks after the initial investigation was launched, investigators searched Roldan's family home, where he was living with his mother and seized his immigration papers, a black bag with assorted documents, and other items, according to a search warrant filed in Fairfax County.

As the investigation progressed, investigators told reporters at the time that Roldan "made conflicting statements regarding when he noticed Bethany's car being parking in the parking lot in front of their shared apartment." Eventually, at some point during the investigation, detectives said Roldan stopped cooperating with law enforcement.

"Some are cooperative, some are not. We feel we have probably interviewed folks in this investigation already that probably have information that we would like to have and they've been reluctant to hand that information over. So, we're hopeful that, as the days go by, that they'll realize that if they have information, no matter how insignificant they think it is, they will give it to us," former Sheriff Steve Simpson told reporters in 2011. Bethany's mother, Nelson, believes that Sheriff Simpson was likely referring to Roldan's family members who were holding back on sharing pertinent information.

As investigators dug deeper into Roldan's past they found a violent criminal record that aligned perfectly with the alleged abuse in his relationship with Bethany. In one incident he smashed a woman's car windshield in a fit of rage. According to investigators, when they interviewed Roldan's other girlfriends prior to Bethany, he demonstrated a clear pattern of abuse.

On Friday, Aug. 5, 2011, the Loudoun County investigators released new photos of Bethany, hoping the images would generate new information as to her whereabouts. They clearly had not yet given up hope that she was still alive.

Bethany was due to give birth to her second child on Sunday, Aug. 7, and hope remained that somewhere, some hospital would recognize her if she were seeking medical treatment. "We're trying to get the picture out as to how she would look today," said a spokesman for the sheriff's office.

The photos released to the media showed Bethany when she was in the final trimester of pregnancy with her first child. A second photo showed an image of a tattoo just above her left ankle. For investigators, it was still the only path forward. "Nothing has led us in any other direction," an investigator said.

The investigation turned cold from there. It was clear that Bethany wasn't coming back. She was likely dead. Weeks turned into months and months into years. There were no new leads and no sign of

Bethany. It was not until 2014 that the case took an important twist- perhaps the most shocking clue of all which would lead many to conclude that Roldan had in fact murdered her.

In 2014 Roldan had moved on to a new relationship with another young woman, Vicky Willoughby. The same pattern of abuse that happened in his relationship with Bethany, as alleged by her friends and family, would also emerged in his new relationship. Willoughby ultimately moved to a new city, Pinehurst, NC to escape from her relationship with Roldan, but he soon followed her.

Police responded to a 911 call for a domestic violence incident at 1:30 a.m. on Nov. 12, 2014. Willoughby had shot Roldan in self-defense twice — once in the chest and once in the abdomen. But the weak stopping power of her .38 caliber handgun did not bring him down. Instead, Roldan charged forward and wrestled the gun out of Willoughby's hand and shot her three times, hitting her in the head and leg. Miraculously, she survived the shooting, but lost her right eye.

Four months later, Roldan was charged with the attempted murder of Willoughby. In addition to shooting her, Roldan also broke Willoughby's neck, bit her, and punched her.

Roldan took a plea deal in the case in May, 2015 and the charges were consolidated into one sentence, with a minimum of six years and a maximum of eight years and three months. Roldan pleaded guilty to two reduced charges — felony assault with a deadly weapon with intent to kill, inflicting serious injury, and felony assault inflicting serious bodily injury.

But with time served, he could be released as early as 2020. The Assistant District Attorney in the case, Peter Strickland, said he made the decision to accept the plea agreement during jury selection.

Presumably, after he finishes his prison sentence, U.S. Immigration and Customs Enforcement would take custody of Roldan to begin processing him for deportation back to Bolivia. But with millions of criminally convicted immigrants awaiting deportation approval from their host countries, his future status in the U.S. remains unclear.

As for Willoughby, she was astonished that an attempted murder case such as this would yield such a light sentence.

"I am disappointed in the gaps leading to technicalities and diminishing the consequences for such violence," Willoughby said. "This was not a first offense. Violent repeat offenders should be kept off the street. I fear for the next victim, in this country or another."

The other offense Willoughby was referring to, of course, was Bethany's disappearance. His arrest and subsequent plea-deal triggered red flags for those still investigating Bethany's disappearance. His pattern of controlling, obsessive behavior with women was apparent. But now there was actual, documented evidence of his capacity to cross the line from obsessive, stalking behavior into dangerous violence.

Bethany's mother had hoped for a longer sentence for Roldan. "There is no sentence that can equate to the terror and suffering caused by Ronald to Vicky and others, including Bethany," she told reporters, "I am hoping that him being behind bars will allow someone who has information about Bethany to come forward so there can be justice for Bethany. I pray that their heart would be moved to do the right thing so their [conscience will be] clear."

In cases such as these, prior convictions or arrests go a long way towards demonstrating an actual pattern of abuse. Most violent criminals have a long record of exhibiting violent behaviors and domestic abusers, in particular, have a history of controlling and obsessive behavior with their significant others, often punctuated by fits of rage and violence.

Domestic abuse is unlikely to end when the victim ends the relationship. In fact, it can often escalate when the abused victim tries to separate. The abusers will explode at the impending loss of control. Many murders of abused women occur during or after the separation, when the abuser feels the victim is escaping his control and he fails to re-establish it.

Research shows that the overwhelming number of domestic abusers are never arrested. Those that are arrested often had prior domestic violence arrests or orders of protection filed against them and fall into the category of serial domestic abusers. Additionally, only a very small percentage of those arrested for domestic violence had no prior criminal history at all.

Investigators never charged Roldan or named him as a suspect, but said he is no longer willing to answer questions about Bethany's disappearance and acknowledge that there are no other suspects. They also maintain that they have no evidence that suggests Decker is alive or dead.

One day after Roldan's guilty plea, on Friday, May 13, it was (or would have been) Bethany's 27th birthday. Nelson wished her daughter a happy birthday on her Facebook page and said, "We have been waiting a long time but will not lose hope."

Whether or not any further leads will develop in this case is unclear. But investigators, after five years, finally filed a search warrant requesting access to a cellphone, tablet and laptop belonging to Ronald Roldan. And buried within the search warrant, was a revealing quote from Roldan's ex-girlfriend, Willoughby, who told police Roldan once said, "I've made someone disappear before and I'll do it again."

So does the evidence implicate Roland in the disappearance and likely murder of Bethany Decker? Without actual forensic evidence or even definitive proof that she is dead, it is unlikely that any charges will be brought against Roldan. But what is almost certainly clear is that Roldan fit the pattern of a serial domestic abuser. The prior criminal convictions, the allegations of abuse from Bethany's family, and his refusal to submit to a polygraph test, makes him a a likely suspect in the court of public opinion.

MISSING JOYCE

ALLISON WOODHOUSE

26

April is a gorgeous time be in Washington, DC. Temperatures across America's capital city steadily rise as Spring arrives and the streets become lined with blooming Cherry Blossom trees.

But in 1999, April brought news of a tragedy to Washington, DC, and to the family of Joyce Chiang.

Joyce was an American attorney who worked for the Immigration and Naturalization Service. She had been missing for three months, and now, her badly decomposed body was being dragged from the Potomac River.

What happened to the bright and beautiful Joyce Chiang?

Chapter 2

Although Joyce Chiang's life ended in tragedy, it had begun far from it.

Joyce Chiang was born on December 7, 1970 in Chicago Illinois to Taiwanese immigrants. Her parents had both moved to the United States of America separately to pursue higher education. They also instilled a love of learning into all four of their children.

Chiang's father Chiang Mu-dong was born and raised in Taipei City, in Northern Taiwan. He had spent many years attending the National Taiwan University, and was awarded with a degree in chemical engineering for his efforts. He relocated to the United States in 1950 in order to attend Cleveland State University before deciding ultimately to pursue his graduate studies at the University of Notre Dame.

Chiang Mu-dong's decision to attend the University of Notre Dame became one of fate. While there, he met a young woman by the name of Shen Yin-hsiang. Shen Yin-hsiang had grown up in Tainan City, a three-hour drive from where he himself had grown up. After finishing school in Tainan, Shen Yin-hsiang had moved to Japan to study abroad; eventually, she too decided to pursue further studies at the University of Notre Dame.

The two married shortly after meeting.

The Chiang family enjoyed life. Both Mu-dong and Yin-hsiang found well-paying jobs, and the couple was well off. They found themselves living in some of the more prestigious areas of the country—first in New York City, where they had their two of their sons, and then later in Chicago, where they had a third son and a daughter, Joyce.

Joyce was an independent and outgoing young girl. She was very bright and was accepted into the University of Chicago Laboratory Schools, or UCLS, where she attended high school, despite her brothers attending the public Carl Sandburg High School. She kept her head down and studied hard.

After graduating from UCLS in 1988, Chiang decided to part from the rest of her family altogether to attend Smith College in Northampton, Massachusetts.

Smith College is a prestigious women's liberal arts college. It's the largest member of the Seven Sisters institutions and to this day has a reputation for providing one of the best liberal arts educations money can buy. Chiang was a shoo-in for acceptance after having attended UCLS, one of the top preparatory school in the country. It had been Chiang's dream school, and she worked hard once she was there.

In her senior year, Chiang was elected President of the Student Government Association. She had campaigned for months and was elected in September of 1991. As President, Chiang was responsible for overseeing student organizations within the Association, and was charged with being a proactive representative of the Smith College student body at large. It gave her the opportunity to make changes for the better within the College, and to fight for changes to be made. Her success in this position was noted, and it lit the fire under her belly that she needed to realize her true passion. She wasn't going to stop her educational career with a Bachelor's of Arts, she was going to law school.

Chapter 3

After graduating from Smith College in 1992, Joyce Chiang moved to Washington, DC. She hoped to pursue a life dedicated to fighting for justice from the heart of the United States, and she seemed to have a bright future ahead.

Joyce moved to the Dupont Circle area of D.C., a historic district in the area. Dupont circle is well-known to be a trendy area of capital city, marked by the trendy coffee houses, restaurants, bars, and upscale retail store that line its streets.

Joyce enjoyed living in the Dupont Circle area. It was a vibrant neighborhood and a short walk to the Georgetown University Law Center, which Chiang began attending in September of 1992. Chiang, who was deathly terrified of driving, often wandered throughout her neighbourhood to and from the University and local coffee shops. She had a favorite Starbucks that was only four blocks from her apartment on Church Street. On Sundays, she attended a weekly farmer's market.

Joyce was a busy young girl. In addition to being hard at work on a law degree at Georgetown, she also worked as a legislative aide in the office of Congressman Howard Berman—a job that had begun as a summer intern position when she first moved to D.C. After her internship expired, Chiang's hard work had earned her a full time position. Gene Smith, Berman's chief of staff, onced described Chiang as "an uncommonly terrific person. She was very engaged, and smart as can be—a special kind of person."

Although Chiang had a great job, where she was well-liked and well-paid, it wasn't enough for her. She knew in her bones she was meant for more. Following in the footsteps of her two brothers, Joyce decided to transfer all her law studies to night classes. This way, she could keep her full time day job while working towards her higher education.

The grind invigorated and energized Chiang. She was the life of her fellow classmates, and was always the one to organize their late-night cram sessions, and according to her friends, she was always able to transform them into something that resembled fun.

In 1995, Joyce Chiang received her law degree from the Georgetown University Law Centre. Unfortunately, Joyce's father was unable to attend the ceremony—he had passed away earlier in the year after suffering an apparent heart attack and drowning in a swimming pool. Chiang had redirected her grief into passion and was now graduating with honors. To those close to her it seemed like all of her hard work had finally paid off, but Chiang wasn't done yet. Chiang quickly moved up the ranks in Berman's office. She no longer was in charge of answering phones and mail. She was now the staff expert on immigration issues.

Chiang's success working for Congressman Howard Berman did not go unnoticed by outside forces, and Chiang was soon being headhunted by other organizations who wanted her on their side. She took a job with the INS, the United States Immigration and Naturalization Service, which classified her as a federal employee.

At the time, most people in Chiang's field saw the INS as a bully agency, second only to the IRS, but Joyce didn't mind. As a daughter of immigrants, Chiang knew firsthand how beneficial immigrants could be to the US, and how beneficial moving to the US could be for people struggling around the globe. She was happy to put her head down and work hard for the organization that made it possible for her life to be the way it was.

Joel Najar succeeded Chiang as the immigration specialist in Howard Berman's office, he was also a good friend of hers. He once stated that he was surprised that Chiang decided to move on to the INS, because of its reputation problem it was often seen as a difficult agency to work for "But", as Najar stated, "there are a lot of good people over there, and she was one of them. More power to her if she can go in there and improve the agency's image and its delivery of services and the way it enforces the law."

Chapter 4

Chiang loved her job; she was dedicated to it through and through. It consumed her life. And in doing so, her job left her little time for socializing other than with coworkers. She enjoyed dating, but found she had little time with it. She joked with friends that she had had a better dating life while attending the all-female Smith College than she had since moving to Washington. Living with her brother, Roger Chiang, didn't help that.

Despite having little time for socializing, Joyce still managed to find time for her friends. "She was the kind of person you want to keep around in your life," stated Joel Najar, a long-term friend of Chiang's. "She had a lot of friends—and she kept them."

Because of Chiang's intense work schedule, the most common form of socializing for the young woman was after hours at the office, which posed a problem for Joyce. The neighborhood around the INS headquarters was less than safe for a woman walking alone at night, and Joyce didn't own a car. She was scared of driving as a teenager and the fear had remained, despite having a license she chose not to drive. According to co-workers and her brother, Roger, Joyce was always careful to take a cab home if she stayed late with friends. That or she hitched a ride with someone else.

Joyce preferred to take cabs—it was less hassle for her friends and the ride was short, only a five or six or seven dollar ride. But the cost began to add up over time as the frequency of her late-night hangs at the office increased.

Whenever Joyce felt exasperated by life, she always had her family to rely on. Roger Chiang recalled that the Chiang's had been making a plan to buy a vehicle for Joyce so she could learn to drive and be more safe without having to take on a huge financial burden so soon after graduating University.

During the Autumn of 1998

Chiang was assigned to a three-month detail out on the West Coast, which including working in the Los Angeles office of the INS and completing some additional training in trial law in San Francisco. At her current office she was quickly becoming known for having excellent mediation skills, and she wanted to hone her skills.

Joyce's trip to the West Coast wasn't all business though. Joyce's older brother, John, and her mother both called the San Fernando Valley home—they had relocated after their father passed away—and Joyce spent every free day she had with the two of them.

Joyce liked California a lot, she missed her mother and brother John, and her hours at work were less than in D.C. It was the first time Chiang felt relaxed on such a regular basis since starting at Smith College what seemed liked a lifetime ago. She was comfortable enough even to rent a car and brave the infamously hellish highways of Los Angeles.

Joyce returned to Washington, D.C. in early December armed with a new perspective on her life. She wasn't sure if she was ready to go back to the never-ending hustle of her full time position with the INS. She was getting burnt out. She told her friends she was considering leaving the INS in favour of her starting her own private practice, maybe even in L.A. She was a good lawyer, and she wanted to be able to help people in more ways than the INS enabled her to.

Despite worrying about the future of her career and life, Chiang was quickly swept up in the excitement of Christmas in D.C. December was Chiang's favorite month, she loved the Christmas season, and it was her birth month as well. Her birthday was always a great excuse to take the time to see friends outside of work.

For her birthday in 1998, Joyce's friends took her to dinner at Georgia Brown's, an iconic southern cuisine restaurant that was often describes as being the soul of D.C. This year, like so many before, Joyce showed up to her birthday dinner bearing gifts of her own. She wanted to give back to those who were kind enough to remember her birthday, and she used the excuse of early Christmas presents despite it being only the 7th of December.

Joyce was almost always on the giving end of favors. It made her uncomfortable to see others go out of the way for her, even though she often went out of her way for others, even strangers. A week before Christmas Joyce had shown up late to a party in one of these such cases. A Chinese woman had approached her while shopping at the Pentagon City Mall. She spoke very little English but managed to tell Chiang that she was looking for clothes for her daughter who looked to be about Joyce's size. Joyce spent an hour with the woman she'd just met, helping her pick out clothes and even trying a few of them on.

That Christmas Joyce made the tough decision to stay in Washington for Christmas. She had only just returned from her detail in California and wasn't able to take the time off work. She was still manically trying to catch up. Her younger brother and roommate Roger flew back to California and delivered Joyce's presents for her. She was missed by the family, and she missed them all back, but they all understood that sometimes duty had to come first.

Joyce took a few days off between Christmas and New Year's to rest. It reminded her friends of back in their college days when Joyce would work non-stop all the way to exams and then sleep for 24-hours after. She spent New Year's Eve at a party with friends, and went back to work the next day.

On January 9, 1999, Joyce Chiang disappeared.

Chapter 5

Washington, D.C. is cold and wet in January. It's the city's coldest month, with temperatures staying in the mid-to-low 20's. January 9, 1999 was no exception to this.

On this day, a Saturday, Joyce was keeping busy, sticking to her usual weekend routine of trying to find a balance between work and friends. After waking up in her Dupont Circle apartment on Church Street NW, Joyce got ready for the day and said good-bye to her brother Roger. She was off to the office.

Joyce worked for a few hours at the INS headquarters and then headed out to the Pentagon City Mall. She had a few returns to make after the holiday season. After that, she headed to a coffee shop to meet up with some friends. Chiang was dressed for the cold day in jeans and a black turtleneck over which she wore a thigh-length green coat, a red paisley scarf, and a second black scarf over the hood of her jacket.

One of the friends she was meeting up with that day was Patty First, a Justice Department lawyer who had known Joyce for years. First recalled Joyce's strange attire on that day, Joyce had looked so cute all bundled up under the multiple layers of clothing that drowned her small figure.

"She wasn't her usual perky self that day," First recalls. " She was tired. She'd had a hard week at work, and she had a cold."

Despite battling the cold outside and the head cold she'd had since New Year's, Chiang decided to go see a movie with some coworkers. She headed over to the Friendship Heights shopping mall with a coworker before heading to the movie theatre to see the courtroom drama *A Civil Action*.

After the movie finished Joyce and her coworker decided to grab a bite to eat. They headed to the Dupont Circle area of D.C. and had dinner at the Lauriol Plaza. When they finished their meals it has hardly 8:30pm but Joyce called it quits for the night. Her friend in California was working in a play in San Francisco and it was opening night. Joyce wanted to call and tell her good luck before curtain call.

Joyce's dinner companion offered to give her a ride home, and Joyce reluctantly agreed. Instead of taking her all the way home though, Joyce insisted that her friend drop her off at the Starbucks down the road from her apartment. That way her friend wouldn't need to double back on their own way home and Joyce could get a hot tea to soothe her throat for the night.

Joyce was dropped off at the corner of Connecticut and R streets on the opposite side of the road from the Starbucks. Joyce waved goodbye as the car pulled away into the night. She likely crossed the road, got her tea, and began walking home, but this is not certain. After Joyce hopped out of the car she was never seen again.

Chapter 6

Joyce Chiang was reported missing on January 10, 1999, a day after the last time she was seen. Her brother, Roger, called police when she didn't return home to their apartment or contact him for a full day. He would've called the night before but he knew Joyce had been out with friends and simply presumed she had stayed the night at one of their houses. A common occurrence. Joyce was reported missing again by her coworkers when she failed to show up for work on Monday. She had been that reliable.

Chiang had disappeared seemingly without a trace. It was as if she had walked into the dark of the night into a new world, and had never returned.

Roger Chiang was extremely active in the search for his sister—he maintained constant contact with the investigators assigned to her case, he held candlelight vigils in the middle of Dupont Circle, and he took every opportunity to speak to the press about Joyce's disappearance. He did whatever it took to keep Joyce in the forefront of everyone's minds.

Because Joyce worked for the INS, classifying her as a federal employee, the FBI was assigned to the case of her disappearance. Their first major clue came on January 11, the day after Chiang was reported missing, when a couple found Chiang's INS identification card alongside the Anacostia River. The Anacostia river was over eight miles away from Chiang's home, not even close to being on the route she would've taken from the Starbucks to her home after being dropped off by her friends.

Two weeks later, authorities launched a search for Chiang or any evidence of her disappearance in the same area her ID card showed up. Although they did not find Joyce herself, they certainly found traces of her. The search uncovered her green coat, complete with a fresh tear through the back, as well as her Blockbuster and Safeway loyalty cards. Her keys turned up stuck in a nearby chain link fence.

It wasn't until April 1, 1999 that Joyce's remains were discovered, finally shedding some light on what had happened to Joyce, or so the Chiang family hoped.

Joyce's remains were discovered by a canoeist who had been paddling down the Potomac River in Fairfax County, eight miles South of where her ID card was discovered. When he first saw the body he presumed it was a discarded CPR dummy, or a dummy that was being used to train emergency workers for a rescue mission. Curiosity had gotten hold of the man though, so he ventured nearer, discovering that it was actually a body snagged in some rocks just above the tide.

Joyce's remains were fully-clothed and appeared intact. There were no obvious signs of trauma to the body suggestive of a cause of death. The remains appeared to have been in the water for some time, suggested by the fact that there was no hair left on the skull. Decomposition and inconclusive dental records meant that it was two weeks after discovery before the remains were positively identified as being Joyce Chiang. A DNA test had to be done to confirm.

Unfortunately for investigators, the level of decomposition of the body also prevented the medical examiner from being able to determine a finite cause of death. Any evidence that could've been found on the body had either disappeared as the body decomposed or had been washed away in the Potomac.

It was a crushing blow to Roger Chiang and his family, who had already been waiting for over three months to figure out what happened to their loved one, Joyce. Now, in the face of limited physical evidence and no cause of death, it seemed like it could be years before they knew the truth.

And years it would be. Six months after Joyce Chiang was reported missing, the investigation into her disappearance and death was officially ruled as cold. FBI Investigators couldn't determine they were even investigating a homicide. They dubbed the case a "death investigation."

Chapter 7

The investigation into the disappearance and death of Joyce Chiang was considered to be a cold case for over 12 years. It wasn't until 2001 when another woman named Chandra Levy went missing from the same area that Chiang's case was back in the news.

There were many similarities between Chiang and Levy's disappearances, which led many to believe they may have been committed by the same person. In order to squash rumors of a serial killer roaming the streets of D.C., police made a startling announcement—they believed Joyce Chiang's death was a suicide.

To Joyce's family, this announcement came like a slap in the face. Anyone who knew Joyce knew that she could not have possibly committed suicide. Joyce had been a ray of sunshine, she was the friend everyone called when they needed cheering up. She had never shown any signs of being depressed, and on top of that, Joyce had been making big plans for her future. Big plans she intended on fulfilling. There was no way.

John Chiang, Joyce's older brother, was quoted saying that the D.C. police's suicide theory "smack[ed] of insincerity and irresponsibility." It was a default theory given after the D.C. police failed to thoroughly investigate potential evidence, leading them to no potential leads.

What little evidence found in the case of Joyce's disappearance also seemed to contradict the idea that Joyce committed suicide. There was the large rip in the back of her coat, and the fact that her belongings were found eight miles South of where her body was. Joyce didn't drive, and so it was unlikely that the young girl said goodbye to her friends that night, walked miles to the Anacostia River, dumped her belongings including her warm winter jacket, and then walked another eight miles south through the sub-zero temperatures to the Potomac River where she then drowned herself.

After ten years and countless pleas from Chiang's family, the D.C. Police acknowledged that Joyce Chiang did not commit suicide. They agreed that Joyce didn't fit the profile of someone about to commit suicide, and that the facts simply weren't there to support that statement. This acknowledgement was accompanied by an apology in May of 2011.

Five months before the D.C. police's apology, however, they made another startling announcement—they had solved Joyce's murder and had identified two suspects in the process.

The night Joyce disappeared, according to police, she was approached by two men who attempted to rob her. Joyce either attempted to flee the men or fought back so the men abducted her and brought her to the Anacostia Riverside where one of two scenarios took place. Either the two men killed Joyce at the Anacostia River and threw her body into the water, or Joyce attempted to flee from her assailants but slipped on the icy river bank and drowned.

While there is still little physical evidence to support these theories, police have remained convinced that Joyce's death was a homicide at the hands of these two heinous individuals. Unfortunately, no charges have ever been filed because one of the men is currently serving a life sentence in federal prison and the other lives in Guyana, which has no extradition treaty with the United States.

While Chiang's family has expressed thanks for the closure of the case, they will never know for certain what happened to their sister and daughter. Her friends will always be left to question what caused them to lose their dear friend, and what they could've done to prevent the terrible loss.

Today, Chiang's legacy is carried on through the establishment of the Joyce Chiang Memorial Scholarship which awards one student each year with an internship at the Asian American Justice Center in Washington, D.C. Even in death, Joyce Chiang is reaching out to support those around her.

FINDING JODI

CHRISSY THOMPSON

Jodi Sue Huisentruit was a news anchor for KIMT, a station based in Mason City, Iowa. On June 27th, 1995, she called the station and told her co-worker that she was on her way to work after she overslept.

It would be the last time anyone heard from her.

There were signs of a struggle outside of her apartment indicating that she had been abducted. She would disappear without a trace. Numerous rumors and "persons of interest" have emerged but no official suspect has ever been named.

Over twenty years later, the question still remains.

What happened to Jodi Huisentruit?

EARLY LIFE

Jodi was born in Long Prairie, Minnesota, the youngest daughter of Maurice Huisentruit and Imogene "Jane" Huisentruit. Her father would pass away at age sixty-two of colon cancer. Jodi was only fourteen at the time.

Jodi was an excellent student who also excelled at golf. She would lead her high school team to victory in the state Class A tournament in 1985 and 1986. After high school, she would attend St. Cloud State University where she majored in TV Broadcasting and Speech Communication.

After graduating college, she worked for Northwest Airlines as a stewardess until she landed her first broadcasting gig at KGAN in Cedar Rapids, Iowa. She then briefly returned to Minnesota to work at KSAX before relocating to Iowa for a job at KIMT.

Jodi was well-liked at the station and immediately became a hit with her viewers who liked the infectious enthusiasm of the sunny blonde. She was petite, blonde and had a made for television smile.

Family members, however, would often worry about Jodi as they perceived her as a bit naïve.

"She would befriend anyone," investigative reporter Steve Powell said. "It was part of her nature and that is what made her a popular fixture at the station. In some of her family home videos, you can see the playfulness of her nature. She was outgoing and bubbly. Not the type of person who made enemies."

"I hired Jodi," said Doug Merbach, former news director of KIMT. "I brought her to Mason City. Could there have been something we could have warned her about and talked to her about? I don't know. What do you think happened? I've been asked that so many times. I feel as ignorant as the next person. I just don't know. I don't want to point fingers at anybody without looking inside the investigation and opening up those books. I don't know. I think it had to be somebody who knew her. I think it had to be somebody who had an emotional response to something Jodi said or did that caused them to do that. I don't think it was random - I don't think it was planned. I think it was planned to a certain extent - but not days and weeks ahead of time."

"She had so much enthusiasm," her best friend at the station, Robin Woflram said. "Every day was a gift and treated as something to explore. Sometimes occasionally she would call, I mean this girl got up at 3 am, and she said 'What are you doing after work?' It's like 10:30 pm and I'd tell her that I'm going home and going to bed. She'd say, 'Oh, Robin, there's plenty of time to sleep. Life is for the living.' And she embraced every single moment."

"It's sometimes difficult to get close - especially women - in this industry because you're always looking over your shoulder and wondering if someone is coming up behind me. I'll never forget the first day she walked in and her laugh. She'll always be remembered for that. She's fun and spunky. I think I'll like her. She's got zest for living."

JODI IS MISSING

Huisentruit would play in a golf tournament the day before she disappeared. She then went to the home of John Vansice and according to him, they watched a videotape of her birthday party that he had arranged for her.

On June 27th, 1995, KIMT producer Amy Kuns noticed that Jodi still had not reported for work. She called her at the apartment and explained that she had overslept.

"I'm on my way," Jodi said.

Two hours later, Jodi still had not arrived at the station.

Kuns would substitute for her on her morning show Daybreak.

An hour later, she would call the Mason City police.

"It became known only after that Jodi wasn't always punctual," Powell said. "A lot of her co-workers covered for her because they didn't want her to get in trouble with the brass at the station. So, her arriving late wasn't that much of an unusual occurrence. Not showing up at all certainly was, however, and they called for the police to do a welfare check."

Police would arrive at Jodi's apartment and find her red Mazda Miata still parked in the apartment lot. There was evidence suggesting that there had been a struggle near her car.

Jodi's keys were stuck in the driver side door, broken in half. Her blow dryer, jewelry, and red high heels were strewn about in the parking lot.

The top of her convertible was dented. Blood and tissue was splattered on the driver side mirror. Skid marks on the pavement suggested that she had been dragged to a waiting vehicle."

"The scene suggested that she had been grabbed while putting her keys in the car door," Powell said. "She was in a rush, having overslept for whatever reason. Was probably going to make herself up on the way to the station when someone rushed up behind her."

There was a palm print left behind on her car which police were never able to identify.

MORNING SCREAMS

Police would inquire with neighbors and found three tenants who stated that they heard screams in the early morning hours. Another neighbor reported seeing a white van with lights on parked nearby Jodi's vehicle.

Three months after her disappearance, Jodi's family would hire private investigators from McCarthy and Associates (MAIS) in Minneapolis who then worked in tandem with another private investigator, Doug Jasa.

"A lot of things struck me about the case," Jasa said. "I still remember all of the cards they found in Jodi's apartment. They were birthday cards. I think there were 50 of them and we're reading through them - reading through them. People had written very nice notes in the birthday cards. We went door to door in the apartment complex - talking with different residences about what they heard. One lady remembers specifically looking at her clock when she heard the scream."

Her family held out hope throughout the harrowing ordeal.

"I couldn't have had a better kid sister," Jodi's older sister Joanne Nathe said. "She tried to motivate me. What are your goals? That makes me stronger. It's a nightmare...not knowing where she is. We were hoping to find her in the first few months."

Neither the police nor the private investigators would come up with any evidence. All they had were more questions.

Questions that would forever remain unanswered.

"What caused her to sleep in that day," Officer Terrance Prochaska with Mason City Police Department asked. "What caused her to answer the phone and rush into work? What was she doing the night before? We all want to know the fine details. We know where she was at. She was golfing. She had driven home and made a phone call to her friend. Those are facts. But its' that gray area in between that we don't understand."

Rumors would plague the investigation as numerous false hopes and bizarre allegations were made. Mason City had a growing drug problem and some speculated that Jodi was working on a story to expose drug dealers. This was an outlandish claim considering that Jodi was not an investigative reporter and was not trained for that discipline. KIMT was a call-in television station. They got their news from the wires and reported it after some fact-checking. Another unfounded rumor came from a disgruntled female police officer who claimed that two of her fellow officers were responsible for Jodi's disappearance. Again, these were uncorroborated allegations and the officer spreading the rumors was terminated.

The community at large would get involved and in May of 1996, over one hundred volunteers searched the area of Cerro Gordo County. They would leave flags in the ground to mark anything they found to be suspicious. Authorities would then comb through the area but no further evidence was ever found.

Over one thousand interviews were conducted after her disappearance. Not one single suspect ever emerged.

Police initially turned their attention to the last person to have seen Jodi alive.

John Vansice.

Vansice was a lifelong Iowa native and lived in Newton where he was married with two children. He divorced in the early 1990s and moved to the Key Apartments in Mason City where he would befriend Jodi.

Jodi would reportedly spend a lot of time with the fifty-year-old Vansice. He was more than twenty years her senior and seemed to be "obsessed" with her. He threw around more money than his listed occupation (corn seeder) would suggest he could afford as he purchased a $26,000 boat in 1995 which he named "Jodi".

Jodi's purchase of the Mazda Miata seemed fishy as well as the car was more expensive than her meager salary as a broadcaster would allow.

STRANGER OR STALKER?

"I was the last to see her alive," Vansice said as he approached law enforcement officers investigating Jodi's apartment. He told police of what happened the night before, that Jodi was at his apartment watching a birthday video.

Vansice had taken special care in throwing Jodi a birthday party. He had printed out the invites himself, making sure his name was printed on the bottom with the words "a party given by John Vansice and friends."

Joann described Vansice as being "fixated" on her sister but stated that Jodi never mentioned anything about him during their conversations. She did mention Vansice in conversations with her mother and alluded to the fact that he may be developing a romantic interest in her. She also stated that she felt "uncomfortable" during a recent breakfast she had with Vansice.

Joann would describe a meeting she had with Vansice in which she thought his behavior was "cold" and "unfriendly." She asked Vansice if Jodi ever mentioned their Dad to him and he abruptly ended their conversation.

During his public appearances, Vansice seemed calm in relaying his support for Jodi's return.

Too calm.

"We're all praying and hoping that she's okay," Vansice said. "We just have to keep praying and keep hoping and I'll think she'll come back. I really do."

"I liked Jodi so much I named my boat after her," Vansice said when asked by a reporter why he named his boat after her. "She was such a big part of my life and she just made me feel so good."

Jodi's friend, Tammy Baker, once asked Jodi point blank if she was involved with Vansice.

"Absolutely not," Jodi said.

"Vansice was questioned by police but ruled out as he passed the lie detector tests," Powell said. "But any sociopath can pass a lie detector test. Vansice should have been suspect number one on the basis of telling the police that he 'was the last one to see her alive.' Making a statement like that, with no dead body found, is a revealing disclosure."

Most people close to the case believe that Vansice is involved but never directly say his name as if they are afraid.

"It is a head scratcher as to why the police didn't come at him harder," Powell said. "It was almost as if there was a veil of secrecy over his relationship with Jodi and what it exactly entailed. I believe that it may have been in part to protect Jodi's reputation. She was an All-American girl, church-raised and church-going. But the question had to be asked of what her relationship with Vansice exactly was or more specifically, what did he have in mind? Did he want to be her older sugar daddy? He bought her gifts, gave her birthday parties, making deposits in the account so to speak. But when he finally came to collect did she rebuff his advances and spur him to murderous anger?"

"What is certain is that he was her neighbor and they would hang out a lot. When they looked into her apartment they would find four cans of sixteen-ounce beers. No way the petite Jodi could handle that and then head off to work. The toilet seat was up. The other thing missing from her apartment was her personal notebook. Most sexual predators wouldn't steal something like that. But again, hindsight is 20/20 and they should have made a beeline for Vansice's boat the moment they found out that he named his boat after a woman whom he supposedly had a platonic relationship with."

THE DEATH OF A FRIEND

Three months prior to her disappearance, Jodi suffered the loss of a close friend named Billy Pruin. Pruin had just proposed to his girlfriend Gretchen Tusler and two days later he drove to Mason City to pick up a new tractor he had purchased. The next day, a friend went to his farmhouse and saw that his front door was ajar with the keys in the outside lock. He called out for his friend, received no answer, then he left.

No one had heard from Billy and then his mother went to his house to check on him. She would find him laying in a pool of blood, he had been shot in the chest.

Investigators listed his death as a suicide but later changed it to "undetermined".

His friends, Jodi included, could not believe that the jovial Billy committed suicide. He had just proposed to his girlfriend and bought a new tractor for a business. He had no reason to kill himself.

When Jodi disappeared, there was conjecture that the two deaths could be related.

His fiancee, Gretchen, was questioned after his death and stated that he often appeared "afraid of something" for weeks before his death.

Jodi voiced the same concerns prior to her disappearance. She written one of her best friends, Kelly Torgelson, revealing that "she was concerned for her safety, that she was being stalked."

Kelly would receive Jodi's letter in the mail on June 27th, 1995 at her home in Mississippi. The day that Jodi would be abducted.

"Jodi had reported that that a man in a pickup truck stopped and eyeballed her," Powell said. "This creeped her out. She felt as if someone was after her. So that is another theory that we have to go on in the case. Because of her position in the media and being a very attractive female, she was prone to have any nut ball start to fantasize and stalk her."

NO BODY, NO EVIDENCE

The investigators continued to grasp at straws while not pursuing anything against Vansice. They simply had nothing to pin him with.

Desperate for answers, the detectives and members of Jodi's family would meet with psychics in November of 1997.

"Psychics would be called upon a lot during the 1980s and 1990s," Powell said. "It was simply a sign of desperation from everyone involved. They needed anything, just anybody with some type of answer. So these charlatans would come in and they would go through the motions. When that happens, you know that the investigators have absolutely nothing."

Jodi's disappearance would leave her co-workers at KIMT devastated. Some left the business while others moved to other stations. Not one colleague that worked with Jodi during her tenure at KIMT remains with the station.

Wolfram, Jodi's friend and fellow broadcaster, would leave KIMT a few months after Jodi disappeared.

"They called me into the office and I thought they had found Jodi," Wolfram recalled. "Otherwise, why would all these people be in the office than to share that information. But there was talk on the internet - chat rooms - he claimed he knew who had abducted Jodi. Gruesome details. Then the reason they had brought me in was the last communication was that Robin Wolfram would be next. From that point on - I had a police escort at night. From that point forward, I look at life differently. I think I used to look at life in rose colored glasses and everyone had a pure heart like Jodi. I realized evil exists right next door to good. It's like a veil. You reach your hand across to experience it. And it's not that easy."

NEW LEADS, MORE FALSE HOPES

Jodi's case would remain in the public eye and garnered renewed interest on the 20th year anniversary of her disappearance.

In a bizarre twist, photocopies of Jodi's personal diary were anonymously mailed to a local newspaper in June of 2008. The journal was eighty-four pages long and sent to the Mason City Globe Gazette. The diary had been placed in a large envelope with no return address. Days later, however, the sender had come forward.

It was the wife of the former Mason City Police Chief.

Her motive for sending the copy to the newspaper remains unclear.

JODI'S JOURNAL

Jodi would start "journaling" after she purchased Anthony Robbins Success program.

Her entries would reveal some of her personal thoughts and how she prioritized things in terms of work, family, and friends. Throughout the pages, she expressed her love for travel, socializing and her search for someone to share her life with.

"Remember," one of her first entries read, "there is no time better than now to begin practicing being the best I can be and living the way I want to live."

Jodi would continue to write about her goals and desire to get the "Huisentruit name out." She listed Paula Zahn and Kathy Gifford as her role models.

She wrote about her dating life briefly, talking about male friends and her love for dancing. She had met a man she liked during a cruise she had taken with her mother. "Why do I get hooked so fast?" she asked in one entry. "I'm lonely here at times and would like to have someone to share my life with. Sure I meet men — but none that really strikes me, or who follows thru."

"My No. 1 goal is to get a new job," she wrote in April 1995, two months before her disappearance.

"I'm recovering from Memorial Day Weekend, unbelievable — Indy 500 — a time of my life. Partied with so many wonderful people — Mario Andretti (world class racer), Joe Dumars (Detroit Pistons basketball player) and Tim Allen (TV star from 'Home Improvement'). Had an incredible weekend."

The latter part of her entries focused more on her activities as opposed to her goals.

"I stayed in Mason City this weekend to regroup, gather my thoughts and goals, read! And have Jodi time. I've enjoyed it. Church is very important to me as is putting myself and family ... at the top. I'm starting fresh at work this week — getting up at 3 a.m. — best newscast in the world — top 10 market — I really think I'll market myself for AZ. — see what they think about my accent. Or I'll move down there to produce."

Her final three entries all mention John Vansice.

"What a weekend, Surprise," Jodi wrote on June 11, 1995. "My Mason City/Clear Lake friends thru a big party for me! At a lounge, wild. It was in Clear Lake. They had a 16 gal keg – huge cake (with a skier) so much left. John Van Sice grilled 150 pork burgers, we were dancing on tables...dancing everywhere...Everyone had a ball. Video camera was rolling, cameras were clicking – oh what fun! Life is so good. The party made me feel so good."

"Last night John,...and I went to the Glen Miller Orchestra in Belmond," Jodi wrote on June 13th, 1995. "I have so many great viewers. People are so kind. This nice weather has me wild. I bought a new Mazda Miata, simply love it."

"Got home from a weekend road trip to Iowa City," Jodi wrote in her final entry. "oh we had fun! It was wild, partying and water skiing. We skied at the Coralville Res. I'm improving on the skis — hips up, lean, etc. John's son Trent gave me some great ski tip advice. Today, Sunday, it was raining in Mason City so didn't get any skiing in. I love it, it's addicting." Later on in the entry she wrote about her desire to move on from KIMT. "Great friends but professionally, I'm fed up. It's difficult finding a new job and I'm confused about agent and what to do."

The journals didn't reveal any clues that furthered the investigation. It remains a head-scratcher as to why the wife of the former police chief would forward the journal to the newspaper.

"The journals said a lot about Jodi's character," Powell said. "Reading through it is heartbreaking because you realize how much she loved her life, her family, and friends. She was on the road to self-improvement and listened to Tony Robbins' success tapes. She aspired to beyond what she was doing. She wanted to make her mark."

NEW SUSPECT

One new suspect that did emerge in recent years was serial rapist Tony Dejuan Jackson. Jackson was twenty-one years old at the time of Huisentruit's abduction and is now serving a life sentence in Minnesota for raping three women in 1997.

He was questioned about the crime and denied ever meeting Huisentruit or seeing her in public.

His former friend, however, stated otherwise.

Speaking anonymously, this friend would tell the Minneapolis news station KMSP that he had met Jackson because their girlfriends at the time were good friends. The source described an occasion where Jackson had invited him to get drinks where he knew Jodi was a regular.

The two then arrived at the South Bridge Lounge where they saw Jodi sitting at the bar.

He stated that Jackson walked right up to Jodi and began talking to her but he didn't hear the gist of their conversation.

Jackson was living in Mason City at the time and was attending North Iowa Community College. He hosted his own student talk show and wanted to pursue a career in broadcasting.

His friend thought that Jackson simply wanted to get career advice from Jodi not really thinking anything of their conversation until years later.

"My gut tells me that he probably did it," Jackson's friend said. "After all the stuff he's done since."

This suspicion of Jackson is corroborated with a neighbor who went out jogging early in the morning. She stated that the morning before she saw a young African American man, riding a bike outside the complex. He started biking ride beside her and she was spooked by him as it was so early in the morning.

Jackson would eventually be connected to over six sexual assaults on women from North Iowa to the St. Paul area in Minnesota.

He would arm himself with handcuffs, duct tape, mask and a gun as he stalked his victims. He threatened to kill his victims when they would not submit to him. One of his victims was eventually able to identify him as she worked with Jackson at a restaurant.

Jackson would write rap songs in prison that contained the lyric "stiffin' around Tiffin." Authorities believed that he may be referring to a silo in Tiffin, Iowa which he may have dumped her body. He had also told a cellmate that he was involved with a kidnapping of a news anchor.

Mason City police would not charge him, however, and it remains unclear why the eliminated him as a suspect.

As of this writing, John Vansice remains the primary person of interest. He has since moved to Phoenix, Arizona.

Jodi would be declared legally dead in May of 2001.

THE STRANGE DISAPPEARANCE OF PATRICIA MEEHAN

54

NATHAN NIXON

Patricia Meehan Disappearance

The story of Patricia Meehan is a very strange and puzzling one. She seemingly disappeared into the night with little reason. The case has remained unsolved since 1989. With few witnesses, the full events are sketchy at best. What is well known about this case is that our culture has seemingly thought of every possible scenario to explain what happened to her. To understand and possibly solve the case, understanding the person that Patricia Meehan was is of paramount importance.

Patricia Meehan was never afraid of change. Her path of life took her all over the United States and to nearly every type of region. She was born on November 1, 1951 in Pittsburgh, Pennsylvania. She lived a typical life. She was said to have been "the perfect child" by her loving parents and by all who knew her. She had great ambition to see the world and to attack life with a smile. Socially she was on the same level as her peers. When she decided to attend college in Oklahoma City, Oklahoma, no one was really surprised. That was who Patricia was. That is exactly what she did.

She studied early childhood development and earned her degree in four years of college study. Again, she was living the American dream and successfully setting up a future to thrive. She made many friends in Oklahoma, even though it was a foreign place to a young woman from Pittsburgh. She took up a career in early childhood caregiving in Oklahoma and thrived in the profession for nearly 10 years. She was unhappy, or perhaps, unfulfilled in her work. She sporadically spoke with her family and a few friends from back home in Pennsylvania at the time. People knew Patricia to take risks. She was never afraid to change her outlook if it meant a new adventure or perhaps a new challenge lay ahead. In 1985, she made a major life change that would, effectively, lead to her ultimate disappearance.

She had informed her parents in the years prior that she wanted to become involved in animal care. She made this a reality when she moved to Bozeman, Montana in 1985. She moved alone. Patricia was not married and had left her simple, safe life behind in Oklahoma to pursue a career as a ranch hand. While this major career shift was motivated to start a happier life, it ultimately didn't always pay the bills. She worked numerous odd-jobs in the industry and could successfully make ends meet on her own. She continued this new lifestyle for four years in Bozeman, Montana.

The last person that can be fully confirmed to have seen Patricia Meehan alive was her landlord. Meehan's landlord reported to police investigators later that she seemed much more hyper than normal. This struck the landlord as extremely odd for the normally mellow, collected Patricia. Nonetheless, there were absolutely no problems between the two in any way. Patricia always paid her rent and was an "overall great tenant" to have.

The evening of April 20, 1989 is one of great speculation as to what really happened. The testimony of Peggy Bueller has always been a key component to the theories of Patricia's disappearance.

At approximately 8:05 P.M. Peggy Bueller and her father were traveling west bound on Montana State Highway 200. They were passing through the tiny town of Circle, Montana. To their surprise, they could see a set of vehicle headlights heading straight at them up ahead. A vehicle heading east was driving on the wrong side of the road. Peggy managed to swerve onto the shoulder and avoid a head-on collision with the opposing driver. The car that had been following behind Peggy was driven by an off-duty police dispatcher named Carol Heitz. Unfortunately for Carol, she was not able to swerve and avoid a collision.

Peggy Bueller had pulled over and gazed in her rear-view mirror in time to see the collision with the car driven by Carol Heitz. Thankfully, no injuries occurred in the accident. The story is very odd and somewhat eerie from this point. Just after impact, Carol Heitz emerged from her vehicle unharmed. She was shook up, but suffered no major injury. Being a police dispatcher, her first concern was for the other driver. The car that was traveling east bound was driven by Patricia Meehan. Patricia was next to emerge from her car after the impact. She stood in the middle of the road, and proceeded to slowly approach the car of Carol Heitz. According to Heitz, Patricia Meehan did not utter a single word. "She approached me calmly and silently," Heitz reported. "She seemingly stared directly through me from the moment she began to approach me."

Peggy Bueller remained in her vehicle and observed what was taking place. What she observed was "one of the strangest acts" she had ever seen. Peggy and Heitz agree that Patricia climbed over a fence just off of the road after she passed by Carol. She took only a step after getting over the fence and turned back around to stare upon the accident. She made no noise or any sort of expression. She stood there for at least two minutes. Heitz described Meehan as someone who seemed to be observing the accident scene rather than someone who had been involved in the accident. After a few short minutes, Meehan turned around and walked into a secluded Montana field into the pitch dark night. This was the last confirmed sighting of Patricia Meehan. By the time police arrived to sort out the accident, the whereabouts of Patricia were unknown. Peggy and Carol gave the exact same story in separate interviews with investigators. As eerie as the accident had unfolded, it had ended quietly and abruptly. Patricia Meehan was officially gone.

Peggy Bueller quickly drove into town when Patricia disappeared into the night. Her father stayed with Carol Heitz at the scene of the accident. Peggy reached a phone within ten minutes and alerted the authorities. When police arrived, an extensive search of the field where Patricia was seen walking away to turned up nothing. It only took police 15 minutes to identify the then mystery woman as Patricia

Meehan after they ran the license plate of the vehicle. She was a registered member of the Bozeman, Montana community and had no criminal record. This was shocking to police who had assumed the woman left due to the fact that police would be arriving to the scene to investigate the accident. This posed the burning question that is still unanswered of why this woman would leave the scene of the accident if she had no criminal record.

Police made efforts to investigate the field immediately following the accident. Police discovered a tennis shoe about a mile into the field that had been accompanying a trail of footprints. The shoe matched what would have been the approximate size of the foot of Patricia Meehan. Oddly enough, the tracks seemingly disappear. Due to darkness, the investigation was suspended until the following morning of April 21. When police arrived to further check for a trail, the footprints led to nothing. The terrain had an influence in this as well as the fact that the actual shoe prints were gone, likely due to Patricia going barefoot at this point in her walk. Police had no leads.

There were two major theories that investigators had arrived at to this point. The first was the most likely. They believed that Patricia had hitchhiked from a small rural road in the area with a trucker. This could obviously not be confirmed, however the lack of a body, further clothes or footprints, as well as a lack of any whereabouts in surrounding cities points to this to be the likely case. The second theory they had suggest that she stowed away in a hay truck in the area and accomplished the same thing. This proved later to be unlikely as no hay trucks were confirmed to be in the field or in the immediate area.

The Meehan family arrived to Montana from Pittsburgh in the day following the accident. They distributed over 2,000 missing person flyers in the surrounding Montana towns and provided police with valuable information. The flyers turned up numerous calls, however none of these would lead to finding Patricia. Over 500 local volunteers searched the mountainous terrain around the accident site in an effort to possibly locate Patricia. For days, people walked the area. Some even brought dogs to perhaps catch a scent trail. These searches turned up absolutely nothing. There was no evidence of human activity in the mountains, and there were no evidence of a body or struggle in the surrounding area. Patricia had seemingly disappeared without a trace after taking a path into a secluded field. Perhaps the events in the days and weeks prior could shed some light into who Patricia was and things she had been recently going through.

The Meehan family revealed to police that Patricia had been going through some dark times in the past couple of months. Patricia was somewhat at a dead end and was feeling lost. She had asked her parents if she could return home in an effort to get back on track. Her parent's agreed, but only if she see a psychologist leading to coming home. Patricia agreed. She was diagnosed as suffering from depression. Ironically, she had an appointment with her psychologist the morning after the accident on April 21. She obviously never made this appointment.

Police also were suspicious as to why Patricia was even in this part of the state anyway. She had an appointment in Bozeman, Montana for the next morning. Bozeman was where she was living. The direction of travel she was taking at the time of the accident was in the opposite direction of Bozeman. Investigators asked the Meehan family if they had any idea where she may be going or what she was doing in this remote part of Montana. They had absolutely no idea. It was evident to police that she had no intention of returning to Bozeman to make her appointment the next morning. But could there be more to this part of the story?

The Meehan family had a roll of film developed that had been found in Patricia's car the night of the accident. The film was fully used. There were numerous pictures of nature. Beautiful countryside and the secluded area that Patricia loved. There were also numerous pictures of animals, specifically horses, that Patricia had devoted her life to in the recent years. Patricia's family stumbled across one picture that was quite alarming. A random picture that Patricia had taken in front of a mirror. She had a very confused look on her face and seemed lost. Investigation of the picture by mental professionals led some to believe she could have been suffering from amnesia. This could obviously not be proven, but would go further in explaining the odd behavior she displayed that night. Some of the investigators pointed to this as a possible reason that she was driving away from Bozeman and was 300 miles away from home. Could she simply have forgotten how to get home? Could her mental health had gotten that bad?

Patricia had been driving on the wrong side of the road and made no effort to swerve. Police drew two possible conclusions to this fact. The first was that she was so far lost in amnesia that she simply didn't think she was doing anything wrong or perhaps forgot the basic rules of driving. The second was that she was possibly trying to harm herself or had gotten so careless that the results were not clearly thought through. These are obviously speculation and will never be proven one way or the other. The mental health of Patricia was most assuredly in a low place.

The roll of film that was developed also proved something else to investigators and the Meehan family. Socially, she was in a dark place also. Out of every picture that had been developed, not one of them featured people that weren't named Patricia Meehan. This is clearly not the norm. Patricia had mentioned that she had had a few boyfriends since arriving in Montana, but nothing serious and committal. She had previously mentioned to her parents that she had become lonely and never really made any friends in her new home. This could help to explain the depression and possible mental health issues that she had developed.

Over the last 25 years, there have been over 5,000 reported sightings of Patricia Meehan. Through all of this, only 3 of those do police feel could be Patricia or are even likely to be her. In the days following her disappearance, there were some interesting leads that were generated by the public calls on the missing person flyers.

On May 4, 1989 just two weeks after the accident, a strong lead was generated out of Luverne, Minnesota. Out of all of the possible sightings, this is considered by police and those surrounding the case to be the most likely sighting of Patricia. A police officer in Luverne claimed to have seen Patricia sitting in a Hardee's restaurant by herself. For over five hours, she was sitting in corner booth drinking water. She remained until closing time, and then proceeded to walk to a nearby 24 hour diner. Here, the officer questioned her. The woman refused adamantly to give her name. She first said that she was from Colorado, and later said she was from Israel. The major problem with all of this is that the officer could not detain her. She had done nothing wrong. However, he left without further checking to identify her. This was perhaps the best chance to obtain Patricia if this indeed was her. The officer left and where this mystery woman went next is unknown.

Another interesting sighting occurred on May 19, 1989. This is nearly one full month after the accident. A waitress at a local restaurant in Bozeman, Montana reported seeing Patricia eating there. She informed police that Patricia at in a hurry and said she had to go shopping at 9 A.M. She said she was polite, but did seem to be displaying odd behavior. Another waitress on the same shift also reported seeing her. This waitress said she was talking to herself and seemed disoriented. Patricia left the restaurant and again, no attempts were really made to investigate who she really was.

The theories that surround this case are perhaps the most interesting in the current media. If Patricia was alive today, she would be in her late 60's. This would obviously make her hard to identify in the general public. This leads to the first theory.

The first, and generally most believed theory, is that Patricia simply wanted another fresh start. She had done this in the past, albeit in a much less drastic way. She wanted a fresh start after high school, so she attended college in Oklahoma City, Oklahoma. She wanted a career change and a change of passion nearly 10 years after she started her career, so she moved to Bozeman, Montana and became a ranch hand. Many feel that she again wanted a career change and a life change at this point in her life. Turning to her parents, they gave her an ultimatum to see a psychologist before she came home. The theory suggest that she wasn't happy with her family about this. She obtained her fresh start by planning an event that would allow her to vanish into the unknown. What better place to accomplish this than a secluded highway in rural Montana where she could simply walk away.

This theory goes on further to explain that she had walked across the field and met up with someone who would drive her away. This theory doesn't sound too crazy at this juncture. The who or why is unknown, but the basis of the theory is mostly sound. Where she would have started this new life is completely unknown. But for a person who was struggling socially, not completely happy, and perhaps not enjoying the rural life as much as she had anticipated, this theory makes some sense.

The second popular theory is the more logical, medically supported theory. The collision that Patricia Meehan had was significant. While there were no injuries on the exterior, a concussion is without a doubt a possibility of this type of vehicle accident. Some believe that it was not amnesia to blame, but a concussion that would cause her to act so disoriented after the accident. The theory suggest that she exited her vehicle with a head injury and collapsed in the field shortly after beginning her walk into the night.

Montana is home to vast amounts of wildlife and has a very abstract climate. The night time temperatures in April in Montana typically are going to approach freezing. Anything under 50 degrees at altitude is going to be a severe situation for a minimally clothed, small woman with a possible head injury. The theory suggest that she was unconscious overnight and perhaps was eaten by animals, which would explain the lack of a body or any other evidence to her disappearance. It is for this reason that the theory is typically not accepted. Even with this, there would have been signs of this happening by one of the numerous volunteers or investigators in the following days.

The disappearance of Patricia Meehan has garnered national attention for the past 25 years. On November 1, 1989 the case was featured on *Unsolved Mysteries*. This would have marked the 38th birthday for Patricia.

Sightings are still reported on Patricia and a host of other in the United States. With each passing year, it is all too assuring that this case will never be solved. The lack of information on the case is puzzling. Those who choose to research the case will find that there is little information beyond the night of the accident and some significant reported sightings. All of these factors have led to a disappearance that has stumped police since that fateful night.

Patricia Meehan was an ambitious woman. She took risk in efforts to accomplish her goals and to get the most out of life. Anyone who ever knew her would say that she was a wonderful person with a positive view of the world. She loved her family dearly, and she loved her life deeply. She confidently left home to discover new opportunities on multiple occasions. It seems that life perhaps got too much for her in Montana. Maybe she just wanted to come home. Whatever the case, Patricia Meehan disappeared in April 1989, and has yet to be found. This beautiful young woman hasn't officially turned up in over 25 years. This tragic case may never be closed. A sure fact of the case is that Patricia was a sweet woman who didn't get in this situation by means of risky behavior or negative interactions. Likely, her disappearance can be attributed to a social low spot where she needed help that she didn't go through with getting. Maybe one day the truth of where her walk ultimately led will come out.

THE DISAPPEARANCE OF KELSIE SCHELLING

ANA BENSON

Every time a woman goes missing or is found murdered, the police usually takes a closer look at their spouses or boyfriends. It is a standard procedure, especially if there were indications that they were in a troubled relationship. The disappearance of Kelsie Schelling is one of the biggest mysteries in Colorado. This young pregnant woman was last seen in February of 2013 and the case is still open to this day.

However, Kelsie's family was quite disappointed at the lack of interest by the police to investigate her then-boyfriend Donthe Lucas, who was clearly involved in this crime. After all, Donthe did invite Kelsie to his hometown on that fateful night and he was the last person who saw her alive. When they realized that the police are stalling with the investigation, the family made a promise that Kelsie's case will not be forgotten until they discover what really happened. They kept the public informed through their Facebook page and eventually managed to reach the Colorado Bureau of Investigation.

Early life

Kelsie Jean Schelling was born on 18th February 1991 in Holyoke, Colorado. She grew up in a tightknit family and later became even closer to her mother after the divorce of her parents. Kelsie was only eleven years old when they split up but she would often talk to her father as well. However, they didn't see each other that often because he moved to a different part of town. After graduating from high school, Kelsie attended Northeastern Junior College located in Sterling, Colorado. She was fascinated with psychology and planned to major in it once she gets accepted to the university.

Kelsie was friendly and outspoken, so it comes as no surprise that she had many friends and was a life of every party. During her time at Northeastern Junior College, Kelsie met Donthe Lucas. He was a star player on the basketball team and the two of them fell in love instantly. Donthe Lucas had a very difficult childhood and he grew up in Pueblo, Colorado which is an infamous place known for higher crime rates than anywhere else in the state. He loved basketball and it was clear that he would be an outstanding athlete even in high school. Basketball players do have enormous salaries so Donthe Lucas did see it as an opportunity to help his family out further down the line.

He was hoping that a scout would attend one of his games and recruit him for one of bigger colleges or universities that had a good basketball team. But his big break never happened. Instead, he ended up in Northeastern Junior College which was alright, but Donthe wasn't quite happy with that outcome. His dissatisfaction was evident even in the relationship with Kelsie. Their romance had constant ups and downs, and the two of them would break up, and get back together which drove Kelsie mad. They did finally call it quits after several semesters, and didn't see each other for quite some time.

After finishing the two years at the junior college, Kelsie pursued her education even further, and she moved to California to attend Vanguard University in Costa Mesa. She was finally able to study psychology full time. Donthe continued to play basketball for Emporia State University in Kansas. Kelsie's family was happy she managed to end her relationship with the troubled basketball player, and they hoped that she would make a new life far away from Colorado. Kelsie was independent and she enjoyed living and studying in California. When she wasn't attending classes, Kelsie worked at a tanning salon with her best friend. However, she did drop out of the college because the school work was a bit too much for her at the time and her only option was to go back home. She moved to Denver in 2012 and started working in a store. Meanwhile, Donthe Lucas was back in his hometown Pueblo.

The two of them started talking once again during the autumn of 2012. It was obvious that they still had feelings for each other, so no one was surprised when Donthe and Kelsie decided to spend the Christmas holidays together. The couple seemed happy to everyone around them, but Kelsie did tell her friends that their relationship was still very toxic. Donthe was still treating her badly, calling her names, and starting unnecessary fights. Soon enough everything will change. A few weeks after the holidays, Kelsie found out that she was pregnant. Shocked at first, Kelsie was lost and decided not to tell anyone for a couple of weeks. But keeping a secret was hard. So she called her mother and told her the news. Kelsie's mother Laura would later say that even though her daughter felt a bit stressed, she was still excited about the pregnancy. Yes, she was young but Kelsie was determined to make it work.

Donthe Lucas didn't take the news so well. Having in mind how dissatisfied he felt about his failed basketball career, it is not wrong to assume that the news about a baby simply solidified the fact that his dreams will never come true. Kelsie noticed the change in his mood and openly told him that he doesn't have to be a part of their baby's life. But it is also worth mentioning that Kelsie confided in her best friend that Donthe was ecstatic to become a father at one point. However, his mind was constantly changing. Kelsie went to see her doctor on 4th of February 2013 and he confirmed that she was eight weeks pregnant. The baby was healthy and doing well. The doctor provided her with an ultrasound of the unborn baby, and she was full of joy. Kelsie immediately sent out the pictures to her mother, her friends, and Donthe. Unfortunately, the excitement will not last forever.

The night of the disappearance

Donthe and Kelsey exchanged several emails on February 3rd, 2013. He invited her to visit him in Pueblo. She turned him down saying that she needs to go for a checkup the next day to make sure everything is alright with the baby. After seeing her doctor on the morning of February 4th, 2013, Kelsie went straight to the store. She worked the second shift and was expected to come home sometime after 10:00 PM that night. However, she was in contact with Donthe for the entire day, texting back and forth about the pregnancy. Donthe told her that she should drive out to Pueblo after work because he had a surprise for her. Not knowing what it is, Kelsie asked for more information because Pueblo is two hours away from Denver, and she would probably be tired after work. He insisted that she would be happy with his surprise and that he cannot tell her anything over the phone.

It is safe to assume that Kelsie thought that Donthe was ready to change and start a family with her. Their relationship wasn't a standard one but it seemed like Kelsie was willing to move past all the negative things and focus on the future. So after her shift ended, Kelsie got in her Chevy Cruze LTZ and drove to Pueblo in the middle of the night. Donthe was supposed to meet her in a parking lot in front of a local Walmart. The surveillance cameras did confirm that Kelsie got there on time, but Donthe was nowhere to be seen. She waited in a parked car for almost an hour before sending another text message to Donthe, saying that she has been in the parking lot for too long and that she would come pick him up at whatever location he is at the moment. She got a reply sometime around 12:15 AM.

Donthe told her that he will be waiting for her in the street next to his grandmother's home. Kelsie is seen exiting the parking lot a couple of minutes after she got the message. She clearly did arrive at the second rendezvous spot, but once again Donthe wasn't there. Kelsie sent him another message asking where is he and Donthe replied that he will be there in a minute. This is the last known communication between these two until sometime before 04:00 AM. After going through the phone records, police did discover that Donthe called Kelsie at 03:54 AM but she didn't pick up. The significance of this mysterious phone call will be revealed later. After reviewing the cell tower pings for both phones, the investigators did discover that they were in close proximity to each other.

The search for Kelsie

Kelsie's mother Laura got really worried the next day because she wasn't able to reach her daughter over the phone. She tried calling numerous times but it went straight to the voicemail. The last message she got from her daughter was the ultrasound image of her unborn child, and Laura wasn't sure if something happened to Kelsie after work, or she was ignoring her calls. Laura contacted Kelsie's friends who told her that she went to Pueblo to meet with Donthe. With no word from her daughter, she called Donthe who picked up his phone and told Laura that he had seen Kelsie last night, but that she drove back home in the morning.

Laura was starting to panic, but she did tell Donthe that she would involve the police if she doesn't hear from her daughter soon. Laura and Kelsie were very close and they did tell each other everything, but she suspected that her daughter kept this information from her because she didn't want Laura to know that she was meeting with Donthe. After all, Laura was aware of the nature of their relationship, and his reluctance to accept the baby. Plus, Laura would probably advise Kelsie not to go to Pueblo in the middle of the night.

Laura contacted the local law enforcement and told them that her daughter was missing. Without any solid leads or evidence, they started asking around for Kelsie. Their first step was to take a closer look at Donthe because he claimed that he was the last person to saw Kelsie. She did travel from Denver just to see him. After checking Kelsie's credit card records, they did notice that the card was used hours after Kelsie's last known contact with Donthe. They reviewed the surveillance of the ATM and noticed that Donthe had the card and picked up $400 from Kelsie's account. They weren't sure if Donthe had Kelsie's agreement to use the card, but that was a felony in the state of Colorado, so he was led to the police station for questioning. He had a lot of things to clear up, starting with the timeline of Kelsie's visit to Pueblo.

Donthe's interview

After being picked up by the police, Donthe told his own version of the story. They did see each other that night and talked until early morning hours. Donthe and Kelsie got into a fight and she felt too agitated to drive back home to Denver. She was also very tired from working the second shift. Instead, Kelsie decided to sleep in her car which was parked near his grandmother's house. According to Donthe, his phone rang sometime around 07:00 AM and it was Kelsie. She wasn't feeling well and asked Donthe to drive her to a hospital. He put on his clothes, got to her car, and drove her to the Parkview Hospital.

Kelsie wasn't sure if something happened to the baby during their argument last night and she insisted to see a doctor before she heads out to Denver. Donthe sat inside her car in the parking lot for two hours when she finally emerged from the hospital. Kelsie told him that she had lost the baby. She then asked Donthe to drive her to Walmart to get something to eat and buy some snacks for the road. The two of them started fighting while they were in Walmart and Kelsie refused to drive him home. Donthe simply walked away and got to his grandmother's house on foot. He didn't see Kelsie later in the day and he assumed she went home. He didn't mention stopping at the ATM to pick up the money during his initial interview.

The investigators did notice a couple of possible leads that could collaborate Donthe's story, namely the Parkview Hospital. Each medical facility keeps detailed records of the patients they treat. After speaking to the staff and going through the data, they have confirmed that Kelsie didn't check in during the morning of February 5th. There were also numerous surveillance cameras all over the building and none of them picked up Kelsie entering or leaving the hospital. It was obvious that this part of Donthe's story was not true.

Of course, the police investigators decided to check out Walmart as well because the parking lot and stores do have surveillance cameras, and they might have picked up something that would be of use. While they couldn't find Kelsie or Donthe entering the Walmart, they did notice Kelsie's car on the parking lot. However, the timeline didn't match up with Donthe's story because Kelsie's car appeared at noon, and not in the morning. Plus, Donthe was the only passenger in the car.

Another surveillance camera which was positioned on the back side of Walmart did record Donthe getting into his mother's car – another detail he failed to mention in the initial talk with the investigators.

Without any proof that Donthe's version of the events is true, they called him up for a second interview. The investigators did have a plan this time - they wanted to find out more about the ATM, and how it fits into his timeline. He told the detectives that he took $400 in order to pay his bills and that Kelsie lent him the money since he was at the ATM while Kelsie was at the hospital. When the detectives told Donthe that there is no record of Kelsie ever being in that hospital, his reply was: "I don't even know what to say right now."

They also presented him with Walmart surveillance video that proves Donthe was the only person in the car. He was surprised with the evidence put in front of him, and before the detectives managed to get him to open up, he decided to lawyer up. He was only charged with the identity theft due to the fact that he used Kelsie's credit card, but the case was dropped. The judge had determined that Donthe did use Kelsie's credit card in the past and it was a normal behavior. However, nobody managed to figure out why Donthe had her card in the first place. After all, if Kelsie decided to ran away and start a new life, she would need the money, as well as her vehicle.

Speaking of Kelsie's car, the investigators took a closer look at the surveillance video from Walmart parking lot because they wanted to follow the vehicle. Exactly one day after Donthe left Kelsie's car there, another man approached the car and got inside by using the key. He didn't break in or steal the car. The man was dressed in black, wearing a hoodie, so identifying him was almost impossible. His body type was different than Donthe's, and the mystery man was significantly shorter. Keep in mind that Donthe was a tall basketball player, so his height would be noticeable, even in a low-quality video.

Seeing the direction in which the car went, the police collected the surveillance videos from stores and businesses which were in close proximity. They put the puzzle pieces together and found a route but they couldn't follow it all the way. One day later, the car was dropped at the parking lot of Saint Mary Corwin Hospital. The man locked the car and walked away. The investigators located the vehicle on 14th of February, 2013 and figured out the timeline. But nobody knows where the car was during 6th of February. There weren't any signs of a struggle that would indicate that Kelsie was killed in her car. Almost all of her personal items were missing, including her wallet and a backpack.

While it is unclear if the vehicle was tested for the traces of DNA, an unnamed police officer who worked for Pueblo Police Department will later say that they did find bodily fluids in the trunk of Kelsie's car, as well as two palm prints. However, no one knows what happened with this evidence and was it ever tested. It is simply another thing which the police investigators decided to ignore in this case. Unfortunately, the whole investigation will be under scrutiny soon after.

Theories

Figuring out a solid theory without too many evidence or information can be challenging. Laura, Kelsie's mother, claims that her daughter was probably murdered and that it was premeditated. The first red flag for her was Donthe's initial invitation to meet him before the doctor's appointment. When Kelsie refused, he knew that he had to act fast. Donthe lured Kelsie to Pueblo by saying that he has something to show her, but he never gave an explanation to the law enforcement about what the surprise really was.

It is clear that Kelsie was alive and well up until the point she met Donthe in the street next to his grandmother's house. This is where the trail goes cold. The activity on her phone stops until 04:00 AM. If we analyze the location of the phones, another theory is that Donthe led Kelsie to a remote location and harmed her. It was possible that Kelsie dropped her phone in the middle of a struggle. Donthe couldn't find the phone in the dark, so he had to call her number. He was very likely getting rid of the evidence.

There is a possibility that the two of them did indeed get into a fight, and that an unfortunate accident happened. However, it is more likely that Donthe planned to get rid of Kelsie, and had planned every single step he would take that night. He really insisted to see her as soon as possible. While it is not fair to put the blame on the rest of Lucas family, the fact that his mother picked him up immediately after he left Kelsie's vehicle at the Walmart's parking lot indicates that she knew what was going on. Pueblo Police Department did stop investigating Donthe, and they claimed they didn't have enough physical evidence to prove that a crime really occurred. But they did receive a couple of noteworthy tips which were ignored and never pursued.

The missed opportunities

The entire investigation of the disappearance of Kelsie Schelling was troubling from the very beginning. While the detectives did not have physical evidence of a crime, it was clear that Donthe was the last person who saw Kelsie alive. In every standard investigation, he would have been the prime suspect, and the investigators would do their best to find more proof that he was somehow connected to the crime. The cell tower pings did show that both of their phones were in a remote area next to Pueblo in the early morning hours.

But there are even bigger missed opportunities that could have provided the investigators with the proof they needed. For instance, Donthe was living in his grandmother's house at the time of Kelsie's disappearance. However, the entire family moved out soon after. The landlord started redecorating the house because he wanted to rent it again. He did hear about the missing girl from Denver but had no idea about the details of the case, or the fact that the Lucas family was involved in any way.

He decided to put the new carpets in and when he lifted the old one, the landlord noticed a strange stain on the bottom. He contacted the police enforcement because he was worried that something bad has happened in the house. However, the police ignored his request to check out the stained carpet, and no one had ever arrived at Lucas' previous residence to pick it up. The landlord ended up throwing the carpet away because he simply couldn't keep it forever in the house and wanted to move on with the renovation.

Another missed opportunity involved a couple of fishermen who were out on a lake on a night fishing expedition. It is important to mention that the lake was located near the Saint Mary Corwin Hospital. As you might recall, that was the spot where the police officers discovered Kelsie's vehicle on the 14th of February 2013. They were out on a bank when a hook got stuck to something poking out of the sand. The fishermen went to investigate and were sure that they saw a part of a human ribcage, as well as a skull.

They were terrified by that discovery and left the area right away. Both of them were reluctant to notify the police because they did have some troubles with the law in the past. But that didn't stop them from telling this story to their friends who urged them to contact the local law enforcement. A couple of months passed before they finally talked to the police, but the lake wasn't searched afterward.

The current searches

Family and friends continued to search for Kelsie even after it was clear that the police enforcement forgot about her case. They created a Facebook group that was constantly updated with new information. Pueblo Police Department did go through many changes after Kelsie went missing. The lead investigator was replaced with a new one who was willing to cooperate with the Schelling family. The Schellings did offer a large reward for any new leads that might help them locate their missing daughter. The reward was $100,000 at one point.

This eventually led to false claims and misleading messages such as the one which claimed that Kelsie was still alive, but was placed into a sex traffic ring after a hired hitman decided not to kill her.

Laura Schelling contacted the police and told them about the message. Since the investigators decided to follow every lead possible, they dug deeper and even involved the FBI. Their experts did manage to trace the message back to Russia through the IP address so it was clear that this tip was useless.

The biggest break in the case happened in the spring of 2017 when Colorado Bureau of Investigation finally got the authorization from the local law enforcement to join the search. CBI did determine that the prime suspect should be Donthe Lucas, and they got the warrant to search the area around his previous place of residence. A large number of police officers was seen around that house during April of 2017, and they dug up the parts of the backyard using heavy machinery.

The search has been successful and the officers left the scene carrying bags of evidence. However, they stated that they didn't find any traces of Kelsie's remains. Kelsie's family released the following statement after the search: "The past 2 days have been grueling and emotional, ending with the outcome we did not hope for. Kelsie is still missing. There is no way for me to convey to you all the pain that I feel right now. Sincere, heartfelt thanks goes out to the members of Pueblo PD, CBI and Parks & Rec who worked so hard on this search for Kelsie. This was a physically demanding excavation for them and we witnessed how hard they worked. Despite all the issues we have had in the past, the new leadership over Kelsie's case from PPD and active involvement from CBI is giving us hope that an effective investigation is finally taking place."

The case is still active and the police didn't arrest Donthe. But the positive changes are happening and Kelsie's family is certain that they will find the answers they are looking for now that the investigation is finally moving forward.

FOREVER MISSING: THE DISAPPEARANCE OF NATALEE HOLLOWAY

76

NATHAN NIXON

Natalee Holloway Disappearance

The tragic story of Natalee Holloway still remains a mystery to this day. The events prior to her disappearance are centered on unreliable witnesses, investigators not following proper procedures, and friends who had left her alone with local patrons. To say that a school trip is never supposed to turn out this way is a monumental understatement. Several theories exist as to what really happened to Natalee. The one, glaring truth of the matter is that Natalee was a beautiful, vibrant young woman who is gone far too soon. Many other facts exist. Witnesses, however, do not.

Natalee Holloway was born in 1986 to David and Elizabeth Holloway in Clinton, Mississippi. Following her parents mutual divorce in 1993, she was raised by her mother alongside her younger brother. Natalee made her life in Alabama when her mother re-married to George Twitty. It was here that she prospered in many organizations, extracurricular activities, and academic niches. Natalee attended Mountain Brook High School in Mountain Brook, Alabama. She was a prominent member in the National Honor Society, was a leader on the school dance team, and competed several sports. Through her hard work, she had earned a full scholarship to attend the University of Alabama, where she enter a pre-med course track and eventually earn her Doctorate. This was all assuming she would make it to the next fall.

Upon graduation, 124 graduating Mountain Brook High School seniors took an "unofficial" school trip to Aruba. Aruba is a Dutch holding in the Caribbean. The group of students arrived in Aruba on May 26, 2005. The trip was scheduled for five days. Oddities of this trip were already apparent. While the trip had 7 chaperones, the students were not expected to be watched every second. The chaperones would meet with the full group of students each night to make sure that everything was okay. To say that these students were taking advantage of this was an understatement. "There was wild partying, lots of drinking, lots of room switching every night," Police Commissioner Gerold Dompig, who headed the investigation from mid-2005 to late 2016, said. "We are aware that the Holiday Inn told them they were absolutely not welcome back next year. Natalee, we know, drank all day every day while there. We have statements that proclaim she started every morning with cocktails. Often times so much drinking that she didn't show up for breakfast on two separate mornings."

Liz Cain and Claire Foreman, two of Holloway's classmates, agreed. "The drinking was excessive. We all were going too far and didn't understand the dangers"

Jodi Bearman organized the class trip. The investigation that would soon follow turned up numerous mistakes and irresponsibility's on the part of organizers and chaperones. The obvious problem was the supervision. How can seven chaperones have control of 124 high school graduates in a foreign place? These students were essentially given the freedom to do whatever they wanted with no punishment. Investigators and parents alike could not believe the lack of supervision and authority displayed by the adults. The punishment that Natalee Holloway would suffer was far greater than anyone could have imagined. However, the fact that this was an avoidable mistake is obvious. Natalee Holloway should never have been allowed to be in this position.

It was May 29, 2005. Natalee had packed her luggage and prepared all of her things to board the flight home the next morning. She had positioned her luggage neatly at the foot of her bed and cleaned up her hotel room accordingly. The 124 graduates had one last night of fun before it was time to head home. This was the last time she would be in her hotel room.

Natalee went out on the town with several of her classmates on night of May 29. Typical of the previous nights, she and her classmates had been heavily drinking and interacting with numerous locals. Natalee had a contagious personality and could always strike up a conversation with anyone. As the night drew on into morning, they arrived at Carlos'n Charlies. This was a well-known bar and dance club in the heart of Aruba. Natalee would last be seen at approximately 1:30 A.M. on May 30, 2005. The story was only just beginning.

Natalee had met up with locals seemingly every night she went out. Striking up conversations, drinking excessively, and trusting strangers was common by several of the graduates that were there. The last glimpse of Natalee would prove to be the beginning of a complicated, international investigation that would prove nearly impossible to solve. She left the club that morning with 17-year-old Joran van der Sloot, 21-year-old Deepak Kalpoe, and 18-year-old Satish Kalpoe. The events that took place after that are largely contested. Through many different testimonies by witnesses and suspects, investigators would check every lead and run into heartbreaking dead ends.

Upon the morning sunrise, the graduates arrived to board the flight home. It was time to start the rest of their lives. All of the graduates arrived without problem except for one: Natalee Holloway. Through irresponsible chaperoning of a class trip and complete disregard for holding the safety of these students paramount above a fun time, an 18-year-old girl was missing. Her hotel room looked untouched from the previous evening. Her luggage safely packed in anticipation of leaving. No signs of movement in the room. Not even a towel had been disturbed. It was frighteningly clear that she had not returned to her room from the previous night's adventures. When the students and chaperones realized what was going on, they immediately notified authorities. Aruban police initiated immediate searches of the island and its surrounding waters. No trace of her was found.

Joran van der Sloot is undoubtedly the most central figure to this case. Van der Sloot was a 17-year-old Dutch honors student who lived in Aruba. At first glance, his baby face and focused eyes would seemingly make him very approachable to anyone. This was, apparently, not the first night that Natalee and Joran had met. In previous nights, they hung out at bars and engaged in behavior not known to most high school students. Over the course of the next several years, Joran would lead investigators and the Holloway family on a wild goose chase that involved changing alibis, secret videos, and fraud. The innocent appearance that Joran van der Sloot displayed was only a disguise for the true monster he would prove to be.

The Kalpoe brothers were Surinamese friends of van der Sloot. Their significance is much less publicized beyond the last sighting of Holloway. Natalee was last seen getting into Deepak Kalpoe's car with both van der Sloot and Satish. This has been confirmed true by both witnesses and suspects in one way or another. There are numerous stories told by van Sloot and other later suspects that bring the Kalpoe's back to the forefront of the case. In such a complicated investigation, Joran van der Sloot, Deepak Kalpoe, and Satish Kalpoe emerged as early suspects.

Action was fast when news reached family of the mysterious disappearance of Natalee. Her mother, Beth Twitty, immediately boarded a private jet with friends and departed for Aruba. Upon arriving in Aruba, the Twittys had started searching for themselves. They located the Holiday Inn and began asking questions. They had obtained footage from the nightclub she was last seen at. To Beth Twittys surprise, the Holiday Inn workers recognized Joran van der

Sloot instantly. He had apparently been a regular in the area. The helpful Holiday Inn employees provided Beth and company with Joran's name and address. Within a mere four hours since arriving at Aruba, the Twittys had already obtained more information than investigators had been able to. The Twittys provided Aruba Police with this information. It appeared that a case was forming around Van der Sloot already. However, the mishandling of the case and poor techniques of the Aruba Police Department were already rearing their ugly head. This case would prove to be a showcase of poor work, bitter disappointment, and investigators being led around by the suspects themselves. The first lead, however, was officially created.

The Twittys and their friends went to the home of Joran van der Sloot. They were accompanied by two Aruban policemen. The fact that Van der Sloot was even allowed to be approached in this manner showed quickly the lack of thought given to the early stages of the investigation. At this early point in the case, the extent of the crime was largely unknown. Hoping for the best, the Twittys only wished to find Natalee safely at the home of Van der Sloot. Joran answered the door and initially denied even knowing who Natalee Holloway was. After being confronted with evidence of their rendezvous that morning, Van der Sloot admitted to being with Natalee. Also present at the house was Deepak Kalpoe, who was driving the vehicle that Natalee had entered in to.

Van der Sloot gave a sketchy story of what had happened after they left the nightclub. He informed the Twittys as well as the two policemen that they had taken Natalee to the California Lighthouse area. This area was near the nightclub, perhaps a few miles drive depending on the route taken. Natalee had been emphatic that she wanted to see sharks. After leaving the nightclub at 1:30 A.M. they went straight to this area to sight see. Van der Sloot informed them that they had returned Natalee to the Holiday Inn hotel where she had been staying at 2:00 A.M. Natalee, who was heavily intoxicated, stumbled exiting the vehicle. The men had offered to help Natalee to her room, however she refused their help and continued toward the entrance. It was at this time, according to Van der Sloot, that she was approached by a tall man wearing all black. Thinking this was a security guard, the men drove off. This, according to Van der Sloot, was the last interaction of any kind with Natalee Holloway that they had. Deepak Kalpoe affirmed the story and agreed with the events.

This is the initial story of the events. The initial investigation is, perhaps, the most ridiculed part in this case. Not only were the men not detained for further extensive questioning, they were completely presumed to be telling the truth. This not only wasted valuable time in finding Natalee, it also allowed suspects to plan their next move. The fact that Van der Sloot and Kalpoe had initially denied even knowing who Natalee Holloway was should have been the first sign of a problem. The second, and more major sign of a problem would come in the investigation of the hotel surveillance footage. While this was obviously looked at during the investigation, this is largely an accepted procedure that is typically done prior to confronting a potential suspect.

The surveillance footage, or lack thereof, was arguably the single biggest setback with this case. The fact that Natalee was not seen in any hotel footage that fateful morning would lend investigators to believe that Van der Sloot and Kalpoe were lying. The hitch in this was that many statements from the case could not even prove that all cameras were functional at the time. The next problem was the fact that not every entrance had a surveillance. This would leave reasonable doubt that Natalee could have been dropped off near one of these entrances that was simply inaccessible to the surveillance footage.

Investigators finally felt as though they had caught the break in the case they needed when a blood stain was found in Deepak Kalpoe's car. Searching the car that was captured on surveillance as the same one that transported Natalee Holloway from the nightclub, police discovered what appeared to be a blood stain. After lab testing and further investigation, not only was this not Natalee Holloway's blood, it could not even be proven to be blood at all. Another door was closed in the initial investigation of Natalee's disappearance.

After the first full day of investigation, United States involvement in the case began. Monetary assistance was given immediately to aid the Aruban Police Department. Additionally, American searchers sought to help with the advanced search of coastline that had been a constant since Natalee Holloway missed her flight. United States Secretary of State Condoleezza Rice stated "we are in constant contact with Aruban Police. The safe return of Natalee Holloway continues to be our priority."

Hours after missing her flight, the media's involvement in the case was tremendous. All of the major news stations in the United States began their initial coverage of the story. With little facts to go on, it was largely reported as a missing person case with no evidence of foul play. No suspects had truly been pinpointed at this point. The news of her last being seen in the early hours leaving a nightclub led several to assume the worst from the get go, however. It would not be long before Joran van der Sloot was at the fore front of the investigation as well as the ensuing media storm.

It was just six days after Holloway's disappearance that authorities made their first arrest in the case. On June 5, 2005, Abraham Jones and Nick John were placed under arrest. To this day, the exact reasoning behind their arrest is unknown. One of the men had previous encounters with the law, while both were suspected of previously pacing hotels to pick up women. Both men were security guards at a nearby hotel, the Allegro Hotel. It is likely that the statements made by Van der Sloot and Kalpoe led police to this arrest. The men were released on June 13 with no charges being placed. This is yet another example of flawed work by the investigation. It was obvious that police were trusting of Joran van der Sloot and Deepak Kalpoe from the onset. This is a largely debated topic to this day. Many wonder why Van der Sloot and Kalpoe were not arrested initially. However, this was just scratching the surface of what was to come.

On June 9, Joran van der Sloot and both Kalpoe brothers were arrested on suspicion of the kidnapping and murder of Natalee Holloway. In hindsight, it is absolutely unfathomable that it took investigators 10 days to make these arrest. The only evidence they really had at this point was surveillance of Natalee last being seen with these men. Aruban police reported that these men were the "prime suspects from the get-go." While this may have been true to a point, police waited until June 6 to start extended surveillance of the men. Investigators knew they would need much more evidence than a video of Natalee entering a car with the men from the nightclub. Aruban Police instigated phone taps, video surveillance, tailing their vehicles, and monitoring of their e-mails. At this point, in order to continue to hold the three suspects in custody, they would need to provide increasingly substantial evidence at different check points of the investigation. With increasingly consistent pressure from Natalee Holloway's family, police decided to stop the surveillance activities prematurely and execute the arrest on the men.

The arrest of these three suspects was met with heavy interest from people all over the world. The procedures by police and the heavy involvement of the Holloway family seemingly left everyone with an opinion on what should have been conducted differently. Many media outlets focused on the timing of the surveillance activities. Having taken nearly a week to begin the activities from the time of Natalee's last sighting, many felt it was already too late to incriminate the suspects. Also, the fact that surveillance started at the time they had already arrested Adams and John was a bit odd for normal investigative procedure. Lastly, many assumed that if investigators pursued an arrest after just a few days of surveillance of the men, they must have captured something indisputable to implicate one or all of the suspects. This was simply not the case. Aruban Police had missed the initial window of the investigation. Many critics argue that in the interest of uncovering the truth, an extended surveillance would be necessary for the time period they had waited to begin. Investigators instead buckled to pressure from an unorthodox family interaction in a complicated case.

June 11 was the first of many highly publicized false leads. Aruban Minister of Justice David Cruz indicated, in a statement, that Natalee Holloway was dead and that authorities knew the exact location of her body. This was all over most any major media outlet as an early morning breaking news story. The United States was gripped with curiosity and heartbreak as it seemed the terrible truth had come to fruition. Hours later, Cruz released a follow up statement that they had been the victim of "misinformation." This simply is unacceptable. As an investigator or someone in a position as high as Cruz was, you can't put the wagon before the horse, especially to national media outlets. What was the source of this misinformation? Lead investigator Gerold Dompig reported to the Associated Press that one of the detained men had informed them that "something terrible and unthinkable" had happened on the beach after they left the nightclub. The suspect, it was reported, was leading them to the location of the body. This, of course, was another folly.

On June 16, yet another suspect, Steve Gregory Croes, was arrested. "Croes was detained based on urgent information given to us by one of the other three suspect," Aruban Police Superintendent Jan van der Straaten informed the media. While this arrest didn't yield much as far as new leads, it did start to give the appearance that investigators were at a standstill with the case. Six days later on June 22, Joran van der Sloot's father, Paulus, was arrested. This was largely believed to be a bargaining chip to use against Joran. While Paulus was not a suspect, as later revealed by police, he was interrogated in an effort to get more information on Joran. Both Croes and Paulus van der Sloot were released on June 26.

It was around this time where public opinion began to focus on Joran van der Sloot. It was quite clear to all involved that Van der Sloot was not being truthful in his story. The events made little sense to the general public. The longer that Natalee remained missing, the more likely it was that she was, indeed, dead. The suspicion on Joran would only intensify in the coming day.

From the time of the arrest of Joran van der Sloot and the Kalpoe brothers, their stories changed numerous times. In particular, Van der Sloot was giving three completely conflicting stories that would put the focus solely on him.

The first story shift came, oddly enough, from all three suspects. Van der Sloot and both Kalpoe brothers all agreed that Joran and Natalee had been dropped off at the Marriott Hotel beach near several fisherman huts. Van der Sloot was emphatic that he didn't harm Natalee Holloway in any way. He told investigators that they were both heavily intoxicated, and eventually Natalee passed out on the beach. When this happened, he began to walk home. It was at this time that he made a phone call to Deepak Kalpoe that he was walking home. Van der Sloot claims to have sent Kalpoe a text message 40 minutes later. Oddly enough, the phone call nor text message was found in Van der Sloot's phone records.

Lead investigator Gerold Dompig gave insight into the third different story by the suspects. This story, told by Joran van der Sloot, was a turning point in that it showed that he was willing to change his story however he saw fit in order to avoid suspicion.

"The latest story came when Joran saw that his buddies, the Kalpoe's, were essentially pointing the finger in his direction. He wanted to screw them by pointing the finger right back at them. But the story simply doesn't check out. He just wanted to screw Deepak. They (Deepak and Joran) had great arguments about this in front of the judge. Their stories didn't match. Joran felt the focus shifting to him and was willing to do anything to change it. That girl, she was from

Alabama. She is not going to stay in the car with two black kids while Joran simply gets out of the car to head home alone. We firmly believe the second story; that they were dropped off at the Marriott. This goes along with the timeline and the stories given by the Kalpoe's."

Upon hearings in front of the judge on July 4, both Satish and Deepak Kalpoe were released from custody. Joran van der Sloot was to remain for a minimum of 60 days. Focus was solely on Van der Sloot as the main suspect in the disappearance of Natalee Holloway.

For nearly all of July, searches for Natalee Holloway remained fruitless endeavors. Investigators had no leads and were consistently getting varied stories from Joran van der Sloot. While police had solid suspicions of Van der Sloot, they had essentially zero solid evidence against him. The media storm updated the world daily on search efforts. With each passing day, reality began to set in for many that Natalee Holloway may never be found. Initially, a $50,000 reward was offered for Natalee's safe return. On July 25, the reward for the safe return of Holloway had increased all the way to $1,000,000. In addition, a $100,000 reward was offered for information that would lead to the location of her remains. In August of the same year, the reward for the location of her remains would raise all the way to $250,000. This was widely covered by the media and many local and national governments. This was a final attempt by investigators to break the cold case open. This strategy had several negative impacts, however. The most severe of these were the wasted time on false leads and folly calls. This was not anticipated by investigators as it should have been.

Between July 27 and 30, investigators initiated a massive undertaking. The pond in front of the Aruba Racquet Club was completely drained. This was within one mile of the Marriott Hotel where Van der Sloot had apparently taken Natalee Holloway. A tip was given to police that was especially unique. A gardener had apparently seen Joran van der Sloot driving into the Racquet Club with the Kalpoe brothers. Van der Sloot was said to have been hiding his face. The gardener informed police that the men were seen driving in between 2:30 A.M. and 3:00 A.M. on the morning of May 30. The search of the pond bed and surrounding area, however, yielded no clues.

On July 28, a jogger came forward with a frightening testimony. The United States media covered this story heavily for several days as it was the first story of someone seeing a woman resembling Natalee Holloway since her disappearance. The jogger claimed that she saw a group of men burying a young, blonde haired woman on the afternoon of May 30 at a landfill. The landfill was subsequently searched three separate times with precision. This search, again, yielded no results.

In late August, Joran van der Sloot became the front page villain to many. Throughout the entire case, it was well covered as to how many variations of a story Joran had given. While showing no remorse or empathy for the Holloway family, the public formed a very negative opinion of Van der Sloot. Anita van der Sloot would provide more material for the family. "It's a desperate attempt to get the boys to talk. But there is nothing to talk about. Joran has no fault in this mystery." Joran van der Sloot's mother made this statement after police again brought in the Kalpoe's for questioning. This left a bitter taste in the mouths of many. It was shaping up to be Van der Sloot's versus investigators.

On September 3, 2005, Joran van der Sloot was released from custody due to insufficient evidence to hold. By September 14, all restrictions were officially lifted from Van der Sloot. Whatever the events of May 30, no suspect was in custody and there were no leads for police. Joran van der Sloot was a free man. The release of Van der Sloot created a frenzy among the general public. People all over the United States and surrounding areas were furious, set in their beliefs that a guilty man was walking away free. The nation was gripped against a common villain.

The months that followed Joran van der Sloot's release provided media cannon fodder of epic proportions. Van der Sloot did several interviews and even composed a book of his take on the events of the night. To the public's astonishment, this man was now profiting off of this whole fire storm of a case. The most notable post release interview came with Fox News on a three night special. Van der Sloot claims that the two were heavily intoxicated on the beach after leaving the nightclub. He went into great detail about the two planning an escapade on the beach, narcotic use, and partying in a fun filled night in Aruba. He showed little empathy or remorse for any of the events. He seemingly talked about Natalee as if she was the villain. Joran went on to explain that Natalee wanted to have sex on the beach, however he didn't have a condom. He left her on the beach and was driven home by Satish Kalpoe. Later, Satish Kalpoe's lawyer claims that Satish was asleep well before this would have happened. Joran went on to explain that he was embarrassed for having left a beautiful woman alone on the beach, citing this as the reason for his ever changing story. He said that he was convinced Holloway would turn up.

This all sat so negatively to viewers. There was outrage over the handling of the investigation. People could not understand how no evidence existed to implicate a man that was deemed the perpetrator. Aruba authorities later claimed that over $3 million had been spent on the investigation. This was over 40% of the overall budget for investigative expenditures.

On December 18, 2007 after extensive efforts to implicate the Kalpoe brothers and/or Joran van der Sloot, the case was officially closed. Prosecutors cited lack of evidence to a violent crime, lack of evidence to a murder, as well as lack of continued funding for the expensive investigation. Over two full years after the disappearance of Natalee Holloway, the case was closed. The remains of Natalee Holloway had not been found. Joran van der Sloot not only was a free man, but had profited greatly from the publicity of the case. This, however, would not be the final chapter to the journey of Joran van der Sloot.

In the years after the closing of the Natalee Holloway case, Joran van der Sloot told several variations of events of that fateful morning. He gave countless interviews, seemingly telling a different story in each one of them. Ultimately, Joran van der Sloot was seeking money and fame through his disgusting actions. In an interview with Fox News in 2008, he claimed to have sold Natalee Holloway in sexual slavery. He later retracted the statements in the days after. It was reported in 2010 that in a 2009 interview with RTL group, he claimed he disposed of the body in a marsh area in Aruba. This interview was never confirmed, nor denied by investigators or Van der Sloot.

Remarkably, Van der Sloot would show his greed had no limits. On March 29, 2010 Van der Sloot contacted Beth Twittys legal representative. He offered to give the location to Natalee Holloway's remains in exchange for $25,000. After contacting police, the transaction was made. $15,000 was wired to Van der Sloot's account, and the remaining $10,000 was given by a middle man. The receipt of the transaction was videotaped by police. The information provided by Van der Sloot was proven false, as the building that he claimed housed the remains was not yet built at the time of the disappearance. Van der Sloot would be indicted on June 30 of the same year. However, he was about to be indicted for a much more serious crime.

On May 30, 2010, exactly five years from the time of the disappearance of Natalee Holloway, Stephany Flores Ramirez was reported missing in Lima, Peru. Ironically, she was found dead just three days later in a hotel room registered to Joran van der Sloot. On June 7, 2010, Van der Sloot confessed to killing Ramirez after he lost his temper while she was using his laptop. Within the same interview, he said that he knew where Holloway's body was. Dealing with jurisdiction issues, Peruvian police could not further investigate the Holloway statement without Aruban authorities.

Aruban authorities were granted interrogation of Van der Sloot in Peru in June of 2010. While he would not confess to murdering

Holloway or her whereabouts, he did admit to the extortion plot on the Holloway family. "I wanted to get back at Natalee's family. They have been making my life miserable for the last five years," Van der Sloot said. Van der Sloot was found guilty in the murder of Stephany Flores Ramirez and sentenced to 28 years in prison. This sentence also included his time for his extortion of the Holloway family.

Natalee Holloway's remains have never been found. There have never been any convictions made into the disappearance of Natalee or any criminal wrong doing. In this case, it would be naïve to imagine a scenario where Joran van der Sloot was not responsible in some way for the death of Natalee Holloway. While Van der Sloot waste the best years of his life behind bars, a young woman with an extremely bright future is still gone. Closure will never be possible for the Holloway family. Perhaps a poor investigative strategy is to blame for the lack of any convictions. Maybe it is the irresponsible planning of school personnel and behavior supervision by chaperones could have prevented this tragedy. Better decision by Natalee herself may have helped avoid such a terrible event. In any case, an intelligent young woman who had everything in front of her did not deserve this end. The Holloway family did not deserve this. We will likely never know the true events of that fateful May morning. What we do know is that we will never get to see the true potential that Natalee Holloway had.

FINDING JENNIFER : THE DISAPPEARANCE OF JENNIFER KESSE

MARY DANIELLE TAYLOR

The unsolved disappearance of Jennifer Kesse from her Orlando, Florida condo in the early hours of January 23, 2006, garnered widespread attention from the local and national media alike, leading to large-scale search parties conducted by the Orlando Police Department and FBI. However, despite the fact that Jennifer Kesse disappeared over ten years ago in the parking lot of her apartment complex, investigators are no closer to solving the case.

Jennifer Kesse, a finance manager for a Florida property and vacation company, had left her recently purchased condo in Orlando, Florida to begin her morning commute to work. However, Jennifer would never make it into work that morning, and her family and friends would never hear from her again. Read on to learn more about who Jennifer Kesse was, about the circumstances of her disappearance, and the local and national reaction to her missing persons case.

Early Life

Jennifer Kesse, a graduate of Vivian Gaither High School in Tampa, Florida, had graduated with a degree in finance from the University of Central Florida, located in Orlando, Florida, in 2003, where she also served as a member of the Alpha Delta Pi sorority. Following her graduation from college, Jennifer began working at the Central Florida Investments Timeshare Company as a finance manager.

Shortly before the date of her disappearance, Jennifer and her current boyfriend had visited Saint Croix, in the U.S. Virgin Islands, for a vacation. After returning home from the Virgin Islands by plane, Jennifer drove directly from her boyfriend's house in South Florida to her job in Ocoee, Florida for a full day of work. Jennifer would return home to her newly-purchased condo in Orlando that evening, the very same evening of her disappearance.

Night of Her Disappearance

Jennifer was last seen leaving the Westgate Resorts office of the Central Florida Investments Timeshare Company on the night of

January 23, 2006 in Ocoee, Florida, after returning home from her vacation in Saint Croix, in the U.S. Virgin Islands, with her boyfriend. Several close friends and members of her family received calls from Jennifer that night, and the last call that she made before her disappearance was to her boyfriend shortly before 10:00pm.

Jennifer typically called or texted her boyfriend during her morning commute to work to wish him good morning; however, he became concerned on the morning of January 24th when he did not receive a message from her. When he attempted to call Jennifer that morning, his call was sent directly to voicemail. Because Jennifer had previously told him that she had an early-morning meeting at work, he assumed that she was busy and would call him once she received his voicemail. He continued his day at work until receiving a call from Jennifer's parents later that day informing him that she had never made it to work.

When Jennifer did not show up to work or contact her direct supervisor, a coworker contacted Jennifer's parents to express concern and see if they had heard from her. Jennifer was supposed to attend a very important work meeting with her higher-ups that morning, and it was extremely unlike her to fail to show up with calling ahead. Upon receiving the call from Jennifer's office, her parents immediately jumped into action. Her father, Drew Kesse, said "We were calling hospitals, calling jails, calling her friends, asking them to call places, calling Rob, and he tried calling her and she did not answer."

Her parents soon jumped into their car and made the two-hour drive to Jennifer's condo in Orlando, Florida from their home in Tampa. While driving, her parents contact her condo management office at *Mosaic Apartments*, located on the 3700 block Convoy Road in Orlando, and requested that the manager stop by her condo to check on her. He reported that she was not home, that her condo was in great condition, and that her car was not in the parking lot.

In addition, once her parents arrived in Orlando and entered their daughter's condo, they did not notice anything out of place or any signs of a struggle. Furthermore, they noticed that Jennifer's clothes were laid out on her bed and that a wet towel was present in the restroom, leading them to believe that Jennifer was at home that morning. Her father Drew later said, "We actually found two or three outfits laid out on her bed she was picking. Showered, shower was still damp. Her towel was still damp. Her work stuff was not there. So we knew that, OK, she got ready for work."

The parents quickly contacted the Orlando police department to report her as missing. Family members began passing out flyers that evening and reaching out to local media organizations, while the local police department began organizing a search party.

A local television reporter and friend of Jennifer's, Scott Thuman, described the family's actions like this: "I made sure they were on every TV station every single night as long as we could keep that alive. They did the networks, they did radio shows. They did every newspaper interview they could." An investigative reporter who covered the case would later say, "It was hard to go anywhere without seeing her face and her picture and also the information on her vehicle."

Timeline

<u>January 23, 2006</u>

Early Morning – Leaves her boyfriend's home in Central Florida to head directly to her office at Westgate Resorts for a full day at work. Jennifer and her boyfriend had just returned from a trip to Saint Croix, U.S. Virgin Islands.

6:00pm – Jennifer leaves her office at Westgate Resorts and drives to her condo complex in Orlando, Florida. She unpacks her clothes and contacts several family members to let them know that she has returned home from vacation safely.

10:00pm – Jennifer calls her boyfriend and speaks with him for several minutes before saying goodnight. Jennifer's boyfriend is the last known person to speak with her before her disappearance.

January 24, 2006

7:30am – Police believe that Jennifer was abducted sometime around 7:30am to 8:00am on the morning of the 24th. She was likely taken either while walking through the parking lot towards her car or while entering her vehicle.

8:30am – Jennifer's boyfriend calls her, but the call is sent directly to voicemail. Jennifer typically calls her boyfriend during her morning commute to say good morning and chat. He assumes that she is busy with an early-morning meeting that they had previously discussed.

11:00am – Jennifer's coworkers, concerned that she uncharacteristically did not show up to work and had missed a very important meeting, called her parents to see if Jennifer is okay. Both her parents and coworkers realize that something is wrong.

11:15am – Jennifer's parents immediately begin the two-hour drive to Jennifer's condo in Orlando from their home in Tampa. Her parents contact her condo's management office and request that they enter her condo to check on her. He reports that nothing is out of the ordinary and that her car is gone.

12:00pm – Jennifer's brother, who lives locally, arrives at her condo complex and begins looking for her. Unbeknownst to anyone at the time, a surveillance camera at an apartment complex 1 mile down the road from her own condo shows an unidentifiable man parking Jennifer's car. The video shows the suspect parking the car, and sitting in it for approximately 30 seconds before exiting the car and walking away from the complex. Unfortunately for investigators, the suspect's face was obscured by a fencing post and neither the local police department nor the FBI were able to produce a useable shot of the suspect's face.

1:00pm – Jennifer's parents arrive in Orlando and immediately enter her condo. They notice that her shower is covered with water and that her towel is still wet. They also see that her work clothes are laid out on her unmade bed, that her makeup and hairdryer are lying out on her bathroom sink, and that her pajamas are piled on the restroom floor. Police theorize that Jennifer may have had a fight with her boyfriend and left her apartment to cool off. They preach patience to the parents.

5:00pm – Jennifer's close family and friends begin passing out missing persons flyers to local passerby. The police respond by sending a detective to her condo to gather information and investigate her disappearance. Police begin to question her family and friends, and begin to organize a search party.

<u>January 26, 2006</u>

8:10am – After seeing a report on Jennifer's disappearance on the local news, a resident at a local apartment complex calls the Orlando Police Department to report that her car has been parked in their complex for the last two days. Police arrive at the complex to verify this report, and quickly haul the car away to local police facilities for a forensic analysis. Police are finally able to identify and locate security footage showing an unidentified person parking Jennifer's car and leaving the complex by foot. This footage would lead investigators to determine that Jennifer may have been abducted.

Investigation

Jennifer's parents, as well as the initial investigators who looked into her case, noticed that Jennifer's apartment showed no signs of forced entry, her condo door was locked, and there were no signs of a struggle. Furthermore, because Jennifer's work clothes were laid out neatly and there was evidence that she had recently showered, investigators theorized that she had gotten ready for work the morning of her disappearance and had left her condo to begin her morning commute. The also assert that Jennifer likely left her apartment and was abducted either during the walk to her car or as she was entering the vehicle.

Two days after Jennifer's disappearance on January 26th, her 2004 black Chevy Malibu was located at the *Huntington on the Green* apartment complex, located at Americana Ave. and Texas, a little over a mile away from her own condo. While the apartment complex her car was parked at did have several security cameras, covering both her car and the exit to the apartment complex itself, the videos offered limited clues to her disappearance.

The video showed a "person of interest" who dropped off her car at noon the day of her disappearance; however, the best shots from the video were rendered useless since fencing from the apartment complex concealed the face of the unidentified man in three separate frames. The suspect was seen wearing an all-white uniform, leading some close to the case to believe that the suspect was a painter or other type of manual laborer.

Beau Zimmer, an investigative reporter who followed Jennifer Kesse's disappearance, described the video like this: "There's two different angles, all surrounding the pool area. But it's very, very blurry and it's hard to see. But you can see someone pulling Jennifer's car into that visitor's parking lot. They wait inside the car for a number of seconds before they get out and look around, and then walk out of frame of the picture. But the next shot of the video was what everyone thought would be so helpful. The next shot was of a person that was walking back and forth along the fence line."

However, he noted, "Every frame of the video, the person is obscured by a post and so you never see the person's face." Zimmer would later remark, "It has got to be the most frustrating thing for detectives, the most frustrating thing for the Kesse family, because for just one split second, later or earlier, you would have seen that individual's face and you would have had a better idea of what happened to Jennifer."

When investigators shared footage from the video with Jennifer's family and friends, they were unable to identify the man in question. A Fox News reporter would later say in a televised retrospective segment on the case that the obscured image made the man the "luckiest person of interest ever."

Both the FBI and NASA were called in to conduct advanced video analyses of the footage to provide more clues on the stalled case. The FBI determined that the person was roughly 5'3" to 5'5" tall, but could not offer definitive proof of the suspect's gender. Despite NASA's digital enhancement of the video, they were not able to provide any additional information that could help the case.

Despite the dead-end that the surveillance video represented, investigators were able to put together several pieces of the puzzle. Since all of Jennifer's valuables were found in her car, parked a mile down the street in a different apartment complex, they were able to determine that robbery was not a primary motive in her disappearance. In addition, a police dog was able to track a scent a full mile from her parked car back to her condo complex, leading investigators to theorize that the unidentified suspect returned to her complex directly after disposing of her car. However, police were unable to locate any helpful evidence along the route walked by the suspect.

After conducted a search and forensic analysis of her vehicle, investigators identified two pieces of evidence: a latent fingerprint from an unidentified individual and a small strand of DNA. Given the lack of evidence found in the car, coupled with the lack of clothing fibers, hair strands, and DNA, the police believe that the car was thoroughly wiped down in an attempt to remove incriminating evidence. The investigative reporter assigned to the case, Beau Zimmer, would say, "There was maybe one print and detectives think that it was maybe wiped down, and that this was an intentional act to not only hide this vehicle, but also to hide any evidence of who may have driven it."

Despite the lack of evidence found in her car, investigators did notice that several items were missing. They were unable to located her cell phone, keys, purse, clothes, briefcase, or iPod. While police are often able to track a missing person's cell phone or bank accounts for clues, her bank account was never accessed by her captors and her cell phone remained turned off with the battery removed.

Investigators quickly compiled a list of potential suspects after questioning her friends and family for clues. Her current boyfriend was questioned and quickly eliminated from the list of suspects after providing a valid alibi. In addition, Jennifer's ex-boyfriend and one of her coworkers, who had romantic feelings for Jennifer and had sought a relationship with her in the past, were interviewed by the police.

One the of the most interesting factors in Jennifer's disappearance was the fact that her condo complex was undergoing major construction at the time of her disappearance. Many of the workers, some who were undocumented immigrants, were living in the complex while it was undergoing construction. Jennifer had mentioned her discomfort with some of the workers to her family on multiple occasions, claiming that they harassed and catcalled her regularly. Jennifer's parents have also stated on multiple occasions that they believe she may have been a victim of human trafficking.

In May 2007, the CEO of Central Florida Investments Timeshare Company, David Siegel, offered a $1 million reward for information that led to her being found alive; however, the reward was never claimed. A $5,000 reward for information on her disappearance, offered by the Central Florida Crime line, remains active today.

Suspects

Ex-boyfriend

Jennifer had recently broken up with a previous boyfriend, and he was reportedly very angry about the breakup and the fact that Jennifer was now dating another man. Beau Zimmer would report that Jennifer's ex-boyfriend became incredibly angry after finding out that she was travelling to Saint Croix with Rob, saying "The night before or sometime before, he had been out drinking and gotten drunk and apparently he was upset that he was not the one that was with Jennifer.

Zimmer would later remark that the ex-boyfriend was cleared by the police, saying "They talked with him several times, and while police say he is not a suspect in the case, certainly you get the feeling from others that he should be talked to a little bit more."

Current Boyfriend

Jennifer's boyfriend, Rob, was initially considered a suspect in her disappearance. The couple had just returned from a vacation in Saint Croix, in the U.S. Virgin Islands, and Rob was the last person who had spoken with Jennifer the night before her disappearance. Police soon interviewed Rob to learn more about his relationship with Jennifer and to ascertain his whereabouts the morning of her disappearance.

However, Rob was quickly discounted as a suspected. Rob had an airtight alibi; he was more than 200 miles away when Jennifer was abducted, at his home in Fort Lauderdale, Florida. Investigative journalist Beau Zimmer says, "The police said that between his phone records and the fact that he was in South Florida, we don't believe that he was involved."

The police department's belief in Rob's innocence is shared by Jennifer's family. He was fully cooperative with the police department and FBI's investigation and willingly provided a DNA sample twice. Jennifer's father, Drew Kesse, said "Rob has been put over the coals, Rob has been polygraphed three of four times, Rob has been interviewed probably over a dozen times."

Coworker

Both Jennifer's family, friends, and coworkers reported that Jennifer had recently turned down a coworker who was hitting on her and attempting to strike up a romantic relationship. Jennifer's mom, Joyce, said that the coworker was married and was refusing to accept Jennifer's decision not to date him, both because he was married and because she did not date people she worked with. Joyce later said, "Jennifer arranged to meet him in the cafeteria at work so that once and for all she could tell him, 'Leave me alone, I am never going to date you. And besides, I don't date married men.'"

The police department did question Jennifer's coworker and eventually eliminated him from the list of suspects. However, Joyce said "We feel it should have been consistent to keep the pressure on that individual."

Construction Workers

Jennifer, who had just purchased and moved into her newly renovated condo two months before her disappearance, had repeatedly expressed concern about construction workers in her complex. The complex, which was undergoing extensive renovations at the time, was housing undocumented immigrants working on the consecution projects, at the time of her disappearance. Beau Zimmer has stated, "Jennifer told some of her friends that she felt really uncomfortable around some of these guys. Apparently there may have been some cat calls and things like that."

Jennifer's parents have also stated that she may have been abducted by a construction worker, with her mother saying, "I can't help wonder if someone was stalking her from afar that she didn't even know. Could there have been someone watching her comings and goings?"

The local police department did question many of the construction workers who were working at her condo complex at the time of her disappearance; however, no leads would develop from this line of questioning. Zimmer would say, "The police tried to talk to as many of the workers that would have been there when Jennifer disappeared, but they acknowledge that they may have missed some people."

Sex Traffickers

Drew Kesse has claimed that it is well-known that there was an active sex trafficking ring in the Orlando area at the time of Jennifer's disappearance, which her parents think may be linked to her abduction. Jennifer's father, Drew Kesse, has stated "My gut feeling to this day, honestly, I truly believe she was trafficked." His sentiment was echoed by Jennifer's close friend and local television reporter Scott Thuman, was said "It would make sense on a lot of levels, as unfortunate as it is."

Reaction

The disappearance of Jennifer Kesse led to nationwide outrage and attention, with coverage in the local, state, national, and international media. At the behest of Orlando Police Department chief Val Demings, the FBI took over control of the case on June 10, 2010 and remains in-charge of her missing persons case to this day. She remains on the FBI's Missing List and they continue to search for her and react to current leads, with the most recent search taking place in February 2014. She is also still considered still missing by the Orlando Police Department, Interpol, and the Orange County, Florida Police Department.

In reaction to Jennifer's disappearance and the investigation into her disappearance. The Florida House of Representatives passed Senate Bill 502, entitled "The Jennifer Kesse and Tiffany Sessions Missing Persons Act," by unanimous vote on May 2, 2008. This bill changed the way that missing persons cases are handled in the state of Florida, instituting reforms such as allowing the Florida Department of Law Enforcement to provide assistance in missing persons cases involving adults. Prior to the passage of this law, the FDLE was limited in its ability to provide assistance in cases involving the disappearance or abduction of adults aged 26 or older.

THE DISAPPEARANCE OF TARA CALICO

NICK PESCI

<u>Tara Calico Mystery</u>

The story of Tara Calico is one of confusion, uncertainty, and sadness. The events of her disappearance are one of the least understood of any crime over the past 50 years. A single Polaroid showing what is widely believed to be Tara, ultimately gives her disappearance its most notable name: The Polaroid Mystery.

Tara Calico was born on February 28, 1969 to loving parents in New Mexico. She led the typical American childhood. She had a huge amount of friends and extended family. Many were drawn to her bright personality and contagious smile. Even at an early age, she was developing into a tall, athletic young woman. She took a great interest in sports and outdoor activities. Among her favorite things to do was biking, hiking, and camping.

Tara Calico succeeded greatly in school. She had a strong interest in most every subject. Her parents would describe her as "the sweetest girl who never wanted to get in trouble". She had earned an opportunity to continue her education at the University of New Mexico at Valencia.

She had also formed a strong relationship with her boyfriend around the time she turned 18 years old. The two were seemingly a perfect match. Instead of movies and dinners, this couple preferred biking and walking, most any activity that required physical activity. Tara's parents enjoyed seeing her so happy. When she was just 19 years old, however, things would change forever.

On the morning of September 20, 1988 everything would change for Tara and her family. She was in a joyful mood. She was enjoying a day off from school at her family home in Belen, New Mexico. The weather was perfect. It was a mild morning and a great climate to get out and enjoy the day. Tara was an avid biker. She decided to embark on a long, 17 mile bike route that would ultimately lead to her returning back to her home in Belen.

She planned to leave at 9:30 A.M. The route she would take would make an elaborate oval that would take her around the railroad tracks as well as the Rio Communities Golf Course. The route had some definite scenic areas, especially the trail along the railroad tracks. The beautiful weather meant that she would be able to make great time on the trip.

She had a lunch date with her boyfriend for noon. The couple planned to play tennis that afternoon. She had made a phone call to her boyfriend that morning and everything was completely normal. Looking back at the entire event, there was one thing that eerily stood out to her family. Before Tara left for her bike ride, she had told her mother jokingly that "if she wasn't back by noon, to come look for her." This was meant to be a playful banter between Tara and her mother, but ultimately could not have been any truer. This was the ultimate, real life foreshadowing that would turn out to be such a nightmare for all involved. Upon leaving for her bike ride at 9:30 A.M. she made her statement and rode off into the gorgeous morning air. This would be the last time anyone would see her alive in person.

Noon approached, and passed. Tara's mother became a bit anxious at the whole situation. Specifically, Tara was not one to arrive late or not show up when she was supposed to. All her mother could think of was the grim last words she had been told by Tara. As 12:30 P.M. approached, Patty Doel, Tara's mother, decided to look along the route she had taken to quell her worries. At this point, Patty felt it was likely that Tara was just running behind or maybe even stopped to enjoy the beautiful day. All that being said, Patty got in her car and went out to search along the route.

Patty got in her car and headed south on N.M. 47. This led to the Rio Communities where she would spend the majority of her trek. Seeing no sign of Tara in the least, full panic began to set in for Patty. Perhaps she had taken an alternate route or had merely stopped to see a friend. As it approached 1:00 P.M. Patty knew something was wrong. A strong sense of uneasiness came over Patty Doel. Something just wasn't right. By this time, she had missed her tennis date with her boyfriend and was entirely too late to assume that she had just been riding at a slow pace. Tara was a teenager who rode her bike religiously. A 17 mile ride would not take near this long, especially with a known route that she had used many times before. Something was terribly wrong, and it was up to Patty to figure out what that may be.

Patty continued to circle the roads around the Rio Communities. She decided it may be best to creep along the shoulder of the road in an attempt to see into the ditches. Maybe Tara had an accident and was stuck in the ditch. What Patty would find would confirm her worst fear.

Patty Doel froze as she saw something laying on the side of the road. It was a Boston cassette tape.

Tara Calico was a typical teenage girl for the time as she loved music. She was a huge fan of Boston. Most any bike ride that Tara would take would feature a water bottle, helmet, and her Sony Walkman. Most often, she would be listening to Boston.

The morning of September 20 was no different. She had her water bottle, helmet, and her Sony Walkman. She had a Boston cassette tape to accompany her on her long bike ride that morning.

As Patty approached the cassette tape and noticed that it was Boston, she lost all control of her worries. She knew in her heart that something was terribly wrong. Patty Doel immediately called police.

An expansive search of the area followed. Police questioned her family to get a sense of any possible place she could have went. Investigators initially believed that she was likely at a friend's house and failed to notify her mother. After all, she was a 19 year old college student. She easily could have felt that it was not necessary to notify her mother of minor changes to her day like this. Patty knew better. Patty suspected foul play. She also felt that Tara was smart enough to have left the Boston cassette as a clue to investigators and her mother that something wasn't right.

All those that were interviewed agreed that Tara was not the kind to vanish without notifying those around her. She had never done anything like that before, and she had no reason to have done it then. Her boyfriend agreed, citing that she had never missed a date they had scheduled and would never "stand him up", especially for an activity such as tennis or anything else physical. At this point, full panic mode had been reached by everyone who was at all close to Tara. It was now a race against the clock.

At this point, police were quite skeptical of the entire situation. A Boston cassette on the side of the road and a 19 year old woman who was late returning home was, in their mind, just simply not enough to conduct a full missing person report. After all, there were thousands of Boston cassette, presumably, in the area. If a missing person report and search was filed each time a 19 year old was late coming home, then there would be hundreds of such reports each day.

Everything changed for police later that day. A policeman spotted a pink Huffy bicycle in a ditch along with a Sony Walkman roughly 20 miles from the home of Tara Calico. This changed everything. Police were now as convinced as Tara's family that something substantial had happened to her. Her bicycle, Walkman, and Boston cassette found thrown in the ditch caught their attention. Moreover, the location of the bicycle being so far from the home alerted police that she had either been taken from this location, or perhaps had been taken closer to her home and the bike and Walkman were simply thrown out at this point. Either way, investigators knew they had a major problem on their hands. They also knew that time was of utter importance if there was any hope to find Tara alive. They would need to work fast and efficiently.

New Mexico detectives began to put all of their resources to this case. They questioned anyone around the seen and interviewed hundreds of people. Being as the route that Tara was to take was so long, they felt confident that someone, somewhere saw something of importance that may lead to a break in the case. Several people confirmed that a 1953 Ford F-150 pickup truck had been seen following Tara just a few miles from her house. This truck had an attached camper shell on it, which would prove significant. It was not known if Tara Calico knew who these people were, or even if she was aware someone was behind her. After all, she had music blaring in her ears from her Walkman which likely would have made it impossible for her to hear anything behind her.

Investigators felt it was significant to understand a bit about the social aspect of Tara. Tara Calico was a tall, athletic young woman who anyone would say was an attractive woman. There were many men who wanted to be with her and date her, and she was vocal to her friends about how she was approached many times by men asking her out. Her boyfriend affirmed this, as he said men had even approached her when they were together. Investigators thought this was significant for two reasons. First, Tara may very well have known who these people were. If she knew who was in the F-150, she may have simply been ignoring them and continuing on her route. Second, Tara may not have understood the present danger by strangers approaching her. After all, she had been approached on numerous occasions by strangers and may have just chalked it up to another guy trying to get a date with her. All in all, police could neither prove nor support these theories without more evidence. Finding a motive or a reason in an effort to gain a lead would prove near impossible.

Even with extensive investigation by New Mexico police, the case really had no lead. The 1953 Ford F-150 was searched for in the area. However, it was not found. Tara Calico was proven to be on the bike trails and the streets around the trails on her 17 mile route. It was also confirmed that her bike and Sony Walkman were those that were found by police on the day of her disappearance. With eye witness testimony and her last known activity before her disappearance, police had nothing at all to work on for the case. She had seemingly disappeared without a trace beyond her bike and Walkman. The case ran cold for almost a year. Posters were put out, local news showed her picture and garnered attention to a hotline number for information on whereabouts. Family members urged anyone who knew anything suspicious to come forward. Rewards were offered by police and family members alike. There just weren't any leads in the case. Life would drag along for the family of Tara and her boyfriend, who was actually a suspect early in the case as police searched for answers. The whole situation was a sad reminder that closure may not come in this case, and that Tara may never be found alive. What started as a beautiful day that was perfect for a bike ride, turned into the worst nightmare for all of those involved. Police, however, finally caught a break in the most unlikely of cases. What would be discovered would be the single piece of evidence that would put this case on a national stage, and would ultimately give the case its name.

As the months dragged on, few within the family of Tara Calico thought any answers would arrive. In June of 1989, a break in the case would come. The harsh reality of this break, however, was that it would bring about many more questions with fewer answers.

It was a blistering summer for most all of the United States. In Port St. Joe, Florida, the heat was at an extreme. In this unlikely place, the name of Tara Calico would be brought to the forefront.

Port St. Joe Florida is just over 1,600 miles away from Belen, New Mexico. The story of Tara Calico had been scarcely seen in this distant place. On a June afternoon, nearly 9 full months since Tara Calico disappeared from Belen, New Mexico, a woman came upon something on the ground in a grocery store parking lot that caught her eye. As she walked closer to the strange object laying on the ground, she discovered it to be a single Polaroid photograph. This obviously peaked her curiosity. She decided that she would pick this photograph up. The striking image she would discover would open the case of Tara Calico up in a way never imagined.

The photograph showed a grave image. There were two people in the photograph. One of the people was a teenage woman, the other, a young boy, perhaps around ten years old. Both of them had black tape covering their mouths, not wrapped all the way around the head but just about ear to ear across the mouth. Each of them had their hands seemingly tied behind their backs, although the hands are out of picture so any further information on this is solely based on assumption. The woman is tall, having very long legs and a slight discoloration on the right calf, appearing to be a scar of some sort. She is wearing black gym style shorts with a grey t-shirt. She has dark colored hair that is pulled back behind her head. Nearly her whole body is visible in the photograph. The boy is in the background angle of the photograph. He is much younger than the female in the picture, and he too has black tape over his mouth in the same manner. His hands are also behind his back, assumed to be tied up. He is wearing a light blue t-shirt.

The face of each of them tell a story. The look of fear is much more present on the young boys face. They look tired and confused and are both staring directly at the camera.

The photo appears to have been taken in the back of a van of some sort. Both of the apprehended people are on blankets and pillows lying down with their heads against the side of the structure. The background is dark, creating an image that appears to have no light directly in their area, rather light that is coming in from the front of the structure behind the person taking the photograph.

In the bottom left corner of the photograph is a book. The book titled *My Sweet Andria* was written by V.C. Andrews. This would prove to be a key clue to investigators.

The woman quickly turned in the photograph to authorities. Upon investigation of the area, witnesses reported that a white Toyota cargo van had been parked in the area that morning. The van nor the driver were ever located. Witnesses described the driver of the van to be in his 30's with a thick handlebar style mustache. He was reported to be slender and of extremely fair complexion. He would never be located officially by investigators.

Investigators quickly noticed a striking resemblance to Tara Calico. Patty Doel was brought in to study the photograph and was convinced that it was Tara. Upon close review and a bit of background on Tara, she had strong reason to believe so.

The woman in the Polaroid was tall, athletic, and very slender toned. This matched Tara exactly. The hair color matched as well as the facial features and shape. The scar on the right leg of the woman in the photograph was also a chilling resemblance to one that Tara had. These clues in themselves were enough to safely attest that the girl in the photograph was, in fact, Tara Calico.

In addition to the physical features of the woman in the photograph was the odd placement of the book next to her. The book was written by V.C. Andrews, which was oddly enough the favorite author of Tara. She had read all of the V.C. Andrews books and was an avid reader. This, to many investigators and to Patty Doel, was the final piece of evidence to prove that the woman in the photograph was Tara Calico. But who was the boy in the photograph?

The young boy in the Polaroid appeared to be between 9 and 11 years old. Investigators initially believed the young boy to be Michael Henley. Michael went missing in April of 1988 in Zunis Mountain, New Mexico. He was camping with his family when he wandered off and never returned to the campsite. This would make the most sense to investigators as is would explain why Tara Calico was in the photograph as well. Both of the victims would have been assumed to have been taken from the same area around the same time.

In 1990, however, Michael Henley's remains were found just a few miles from the area that the family had been camping. It was determined that he died from exposure to the elements after presumably becoming lost in the wilderness of the area and not being able to find his way back. This was a turning point in the case as it raised doubts in the investigators minds as to the true identity of the people in the photograph.

Another problem that investigators had with the photograph was the legitimacy of the photo itself. Several people claimed that the Polaroid appeared staged. While this is a grim thought that is a terrible thing to assume, it was in fact a reality of the times. Singer Marilyn Manson famously set photos similar to this out randomly in this area as a prank. Most investigators, however, felt this photo was legitimate and not in any way staged.

Joel Nugent believed the photo to be entirely genuine. Joel Nugent was the lead investigator of the Florida case as a part of the Gulf County Sheriff's Department.

"It obviously is two kids with terror written all over them. It's kind of a bad time when you have to look at something like that and wonder. No one knows for sure if the picture was a setup. Some people think it was a stage photograph, but it was a real look of fear for me."

On September 20, 1989 *Unsolved Mysteries* aired a special on the Tara Calico disappearance. It marked the one year anniversary of her disappearance. Months prior, in July 1989, a special on Tara was aired on *A Current Affair.* Additionally, as the months turned into years, and the years turned in to decades, the story of Tara Calico was shown to a National audience on several other venues including *48 hours* and *America's Most Wanted.* With all of the exposure came an influx of tips and leads for investigators to sort through. The case of the disappearance of Tara Calico remained unsolved with no credible leads. The investigation was entirely cold.

It was not until 2008, nearly 20 years since Tara had disappeared, that this case would return to the fore front of the media. Valencia County, New Mexico Sheriff Renee Rivera released a statement claiming that he knew exactly what had happened to Tara. The problem, however, that he indicated is that the body of Tara Calico had never been found. This would make it impossible to bring those responsible, or at least who he felt was responsible, to justice.

"The individuals who did harm to Tara knew who she was. They knew who she was, and they are all local individuals. And I believe that the parents of the attackers were some of the people that helped the individuals with hiding the truth or hiding the body or trying to escape persecution," Rivera said.

Rivera never gave the suspects names. Rivera did, however, give his belief on what happened to Tara. Sheriff Rivera claims that two teenagers, roughly the same age as Tara, were involved in the crime. He also believed that several of the men's family members helped to cover up the crime.

"You know it's very frustrating, being that there's a lot of people who know what happened," Rivera said. "They know the whereabouts of the body or the remains. I believe that the body is somewhere very close. The body is somewhere very nearby."

Rivera had been approached by many informants over the previous couple of years. The informants all shared similar stories to what really happened to Tara Calico. According to the informants and Renee Rivera's statements, Tara never made it more than a few miles from her house on September 20, 1989. She was struck by the two teenagers who were driving a pickup truck. Rather than alert authorities and handle the situation the right way, the boys told their families and the families helped to bury the body of Tara Calico. The informants attest that the intention was not to hit Tara Calico, but to approach her while she was on her bike.

"She was really pretty young girl. She was very athletic, and a lot of guys wanted to talk to her, they wanted to meet her, they wanted to go out with her. And while she was riding her bike, they went up to try to talk to her, try to grab her, whatever, while she was on the bike," Rivera said.

Many people have questioned the basis of Sheriff Rivera's claims. While the claims do make sense and would line up with the evidence that investigators had uncovered, why is it 20 years later that the Sheriff would come out and voice these claims. If Rivera had such strong reason to make these allegations and had informants that were willing to speak as to what happened, why has there been no conviction? This is a question that remains to be answered.

Sadly, in 2006, Patty Doel, the mother of Tara Calico, passed away. She dealt with such a heavy heart and severe burden since Tara's disappearance in 1989. She passed away never knowing the truth as to what happened to Tara on the fateful day. Tara's father passed away in 2002 as well. Tara Calico's family never recovered from that dreadful morning, and never got the answers they needed for any sort of effort of closure. Tara's family is still searching for the truth of the events of that day. Thanks to social media, there are thousands of people nationwide that have joined in to find any answers or leads that may result in the truth.

The identity of the boy in the photograph still remains a mystery as well. The fact that neither victim in the photograph has ever been fully confirmed or identified remains a great mystery. While most every investigator will attest that woman in the photograph is indeed Tara Calico, there is no way to match an identity without the actual DNA evidence.

The story of Tara Calico is undeniably tragic. The truth is largely unknown. There have been no arrest and no attempts at arrest in the years since the horrific disappearance. While many believe the overall story that Sheriff Rivera told as to what had really happened to Tara, there has been no attempts to convict anyone of the heinous crime. The only true fact of this case is that a promising future was cut short while she was enjoying a beautiful September day. Perhaps one day the mystery of Tara Calico will be fully understood. Perhaps one day justice will come forth and healing can begin.

www.ingramcontent.com/pod-product-compliance
Lightning Source LLC
Chambersburg PA
CBHW061348160726
47995CB00001B/222